Part

THE BODY

THE NOTEBOOKS OF PAUL BRUNTON
(VOLUME 4)

Part 2:
THE BODY

PAUL BRUNTON
(1898–1981)

An in-depth study of
category number five
from the notebooks

Published for the
PAUL BRUNTON PHILOSOPHIC FOUNDATION
by Larson Publications

International Standard Book Number (cloth) 0-943914-18-3
International Standard Book Number (Part 1, paper) 0-943914-19-1
International Standard Book Number (Part 2, paper) 0-943914-20-5
International Standard Book Number (series, cloth) 0-943914-17-5
International Standard Book Number (series, paper) 0-943914-23-X
Library of Congress Catalog Card Number (cloth): 86-81949
Library of Congress Catalog Card Number (paper): 86-81950

Manufactured in the United States of America

Published for the
Paul Brunton Philosophic Foundation
by
Larson Publications
4936 Route 414
Burdett, New York 14818

2   4   6   8   10   9   7   5   3

The works of Paul Brunton

A Search in Secret India
The Secret Path
A Search in Secret Egypt
A Message from Arunachala
A Hermit in the Himalayas
The Quest of the Overself
The Inner Reality
(*also titled* Discover Yourself)
Indian Philosophy and Modern Culture
The Hidden Teaching Beyond Yoga
The Wisdom of the Overself
The Spiritual Crisis of Man

Published posthumously

Essays on the Quest

The Notebooks of Paul Brunton

volume 1: Perspectives
volume 2: The Quest
volume 3: Practices for the Quest
           Relax and Retreat
volume 4: Meditation
           The Body
volume 5: Emotions and Ethics
           The Intellect
volume 6: The Ego
           From Birth to Rebirth
volume 7: Healing of the Self
           The Negatives
volume 8: Reflections on My
           Life and Writings
volume 9: Human Experience
           The Arts in Culture
volume 10: The Orient

(*continued next page*)

CONTENTS

EDITORS' INTRODUCTION

Volume four in *The Notebooks of Paul Brunton* presents, in depth and detail, the fourth and fifth of the major topics in the personal notebooks Dr. Paul Brunton (1898–1981) reserved for posthumous publication. Bound together as a single volume in the hardcover edition, these two topics (*Meditation* and *The Body*) are published separately in softcover. *Meditation* is Volume 4, Part 1, and *The Body* is Volume 4, Part 2.

Part 2, *The Body*, is a balanced course in perceiving and perfecting the physical body's potential to become an outward expression of the divine force within. All its exercises, breathings, hygienic and dietary suggestions have a twofold intention: (1) to make easier one's progress in the development of intuition and the deepening of meditation, and (2) to assure physical, psychological, and spiritual safety in the process of awakening and directing the spirit-energy dormant within the unregenerated physical organism. With the ultimate goal of successfully transmuting the energy that appears (on its lowest level) as sexuality, it presents a sane and effective graduated sexual ethic corresponding to individual levels of development and spiritual commitment. It also explores and compares some of the differing problems and advantages, with respect to spiritual practice and development, that nature bestows along with the biological organization distinguishing men and women.

With respect to this last point, it is advisable to establish a context for individual paras or sentences in the text that may evoke inappropriate responses in some readers. The material on this issue has been thoughtfully reviewed by numerous readers of both genders. What remains that may seem critical of either gender is being published because those readers found the remarks directed toward specific problems of their own biological gender to be very helpful in understanding—and in some cases freeing them from anxiety about—difficulties which they have experienced in their own practice. It should also be observed that these remarks are made by a widely travelled individual with a global perspective on spiritual practice. That some of them may not be entirely applicable in some parts of the American and western European cultures does not yet thereby invalidate them. Finally, the more essential point behind them, the point not to be missed or misunderstood, is that neither intellectual metaphysics nor devotional mysticism by itself constitutes the philosophical goal of the spiritual quest. Regardless of which of these two aspects one's disposition favors, only the harmonious complementary development and creative union of both these sides of the human nature issues in that ultimate goal.

With respect to the exercises, purifications, and dietary recommendations in *The Body*, it is, of course, necessary to point out that no one with any condition requiring a physician's attention should undertake any program of exercise, diet, or physical purification without qualified medical supervision. P.B. has written several warnings into this category of *The Notebooks*, the publisher has highlighted many of them, and the reader should give them due regard.

Editorial conventions with regard to the quantity of material chosen, as with regard to spelling, capitalization, hyphenation, and other copy-editing considerations, are the same as stated in introductions to earlier volumes. Likewise, (P) at the end of a para indicates that it is one of the relatively few paras we felt it necessary to repeat here from *Perspectives*, the introductory survey volume to this series.

It is a great pleasure to see yet another volume of this series going to press—one that carries with it still more profound appreciation of the dedicated work and support of our many friends and co-workers at Wisdom's Goldenrod and The Paul Brunton Philosophic Foundation, as well as of the many favourable and helpful responses from readers equally pleased with the progress of *The Notebooks*. Information about forthcoming publications may be obtained by writing the

Paul Brunton Philosophic Foundation
P.O. Box 89
Hector, NY 14841

Part 2:

THE BODY

No one with any condition requiring a physician's attention should undertake any program of exercise, diet, or other physical purification without fully qualified medical supervision. Readers should give special attention to the author's warnings on pages 13, 68, 74, 75, 95–96, and 105.

In the human body there is at one and the same time a projection of the Overself and a channel for it. The wisdom and intelligence which have gone into and are hidden behind the whole universe have gone into the human body, too. To ignore it, as some mystics try to do—and vainly—or to deny its existence, as others even more foolishly do, is to ignore God and deny the soul. The student of philosophy cannot do that. His outlook must be an integral one, must take in what is the very basis of his earthly existence, must be a balanced one.

1

PREFATORY

Those who read *The Spiritual Crisis of Man* will remember that I brought the book to a close with chapters which depicted the portals of the Quest but which did not penetrate far beyond them. There was no attempt to venture an explanation in any detail at all of the physical aids which I hinted could make markedly easier the systematic reform and uplift of the seeker's mental and emotional life, nor was there any elaboration upon the bodily pressures, tensions, abstentions, and cleansings which I merely mentioned could help to re-educate instinct and appetite, nerves and passions.

Here the attempt has been made; I have tried to give those explanations and elaborations. The fact that there are practical benefits from the use of these methods is only incidental to my purpose.

The other material is devoted to psychological, emotional, and spiritual work connected with the Quest of the Overself—work that makes it a life of unceasing self-improvement. Out of the wide personal study and the continual observation of numerous cases throughout the world, I have tried to give helpful counsel and to discuss problems from the seeker's point of view. At some time or other, everyone has to deal with such matters as the place of prayer, difficulties in meditation, the life of activity, and the management of desire. Questions have often been asked me about them and the various other topics touched upon. The answers given here have been clearly defined so that they shall afford help for those otherwise unguided. The problems and situations, the principles and teachings have been illumined by actual illustration taken from personal widely scattered case histories. The exercises, of which many have been given, have been drawn both from ancient traditions and practical modern experience.

Every aspiring student who ventures to try to bring the Quest into application finds himself at times faced with problems which generations of seekers before him have also had to face. How to handle these problems successfully is something which he cannot too easily attain since competent personal instruction is hard to come by in these days. I have tried to discuss the problems—covering a very wide ground—which have been brought to my attention during the past quarter-century.

Some may express surprise or even criticism that any space at all, let alone a few chapters, should have been given to purely physical topics and exercises: surprise because the topics seem unrelated to the mystical and the metaphysical ones of earlier books; criticism because the exercises seem to drag the student's mind down to the very material plane which he is trying to transcend. Yet it was a loincloth-clad teacher named Kartiswami, whom I discovered in a curious artificial underground cave only twelve miles distant from Ramana Maharshi of South India, a cave which he had had burrowed out and constructed for him, who maintained most emphatically that the Yoga of Physical Control was the proper foundation for the Yoga of Spiritual Development, and the proper beginning of it.

And it was no less a mystic than Ramana Maharshi himself who, without going to Kartiswami's obvious extreme, thought that some attention to physical regimes ought to be allied to the mental ones. When my book *The Secret Path* was printed many years ago, I sent one of the first copies to the Maharshi. Eight months later, I arrived in India for another extended visit, during part of which I went to stay with him. He told me he had read the book and had strongly recommended it to English-speaking Indians of the modern educated class, those who had little mystical faith or knowledge left in them. "However," he added, "there is one defect in it." I asked him to tell me what that was, and then he uttered this criticism: "It is not complete. It should have had a chapter on dietary restrictions. The Westerner should be told that his habits of eating meat, drinking intoxicating liquor, and smoking tobacco—whatever effect they have on the ordinary man—bring impurities into the mind and make meditation more difficult for the spiritually aspiring man." I immediately accepted his criticism but explained that the omission was deliberate. In those years it seemed to me more important to awaken the Westerner to take a little sympathetic interest in the practice of meditation than it was to arouse his swift antagonism by attacking some of his most familiar daily habits. I felt sure that this could be done.

How far I succeeded in the first objective was the subject of appreciative comment by the late Margaret Wilson, daughter of the celebrated former president of the United States. She once expressed the belief that as regards initiation into meditation I had given a real message to the West. It was an undeniable fact that when I first began to write on the subject it was a little known art to most Occidentals, however familiar it was to the Orientals. In Europe and America, it was known principally in Catholic monasteries and convents, Quaker meeting houses, and Theosophical lodges. But an immense multitude of lay folk, whatever their religion, knew nothing of it, or knew only the name. That was more than a quarter-century ago. I then publicly stated that restoration of its practice to an honoured place was an important need in modern life. How contrasting is the situation today! Secluded, noise-proofed rooms where those who wish can meditate or pray without any interruption or outside distraction have been constructed and opened in the United Nations headquarters for the use of delegates and the staff, at the United States Capitol for the use of congressmen and senators, and at the Massachusetts Institute of Technology for the use of faculty and students. At the Hotel New Yorker, special rooms are open twenty-four hours a day for those persons desiring moments of contemplation and prayer. During a critical time of the war, B.B.C., the British Broadcasting Corporation, was persuaded to institute a "Silent Minute" period on its evening program which called for a quiet pause in the nation's affairs to be used in meditation or prayer. There are now several churches in England and America where the sign "Open for Prayer and Meditation" is prominently displayed, and where the doors are kept open for this special purpose beyond the usual service hours.

As regards the second objective which was the subject of Maharshi's allusion, the fact is that my researches into religious, mystical, and philosophic subjects have been of so many-sided a character that no narrow result could ultimately emerge from them. For instance, it will be noticed that I have drawn contributions from Oriental knowledge and practice, including the less-known systems of Indian yoga, but I have not limited myself to the Oriental systems. Indeed, it has been my aim to create a synthesis of them with the best of our own Occidental knowledge and practice. Such a synthesis is essential for those who wish to achieve the highest success in their endeavours, and I consider it will have to be made eventually—not only by those who follow the Quest but by the leaders of Western culture itself.

How then, with such a broad aim in view, could I have failed to cover the subject of physical yoga during the years of my researches? More than twenty years ago, I published some articles about it in a British journal and even proposed to write a short book on the subject. But the publishers did not think there was sufficient public interest to justify their risk so the proposal was dropped. It was ahead of its time then, but there is no question that its time has now arrived. The interest in Oriental culture, which began as an interest in Oriental art, furniture, porcelain, and teas as early as the seventeenth and eighteenth centuries, was followed by the interest in Oriental religion and philosophy which began in the last quarter of the last century. An interest in Oriental mental hygiene developed during the second quarter of this century. The present interest in Oriental physical culture and physical hygiene started in several European countries a few years ago and has now spread to America. But it is only an early ripple of a large wave that will come later, when those who have benefitted by them begin to share the enthusiasm with others. It will not only develop further but, along with the interest in dieting for purposes of weight reduction, in America and Europe these waves will in time ripple far beyond bodily concerns. They will not only fulfil their obvious and immediate function but, as in the case of the Oriental physical hygiene, will also fulfil a deeper function than relieving ailments, improving health, and increasing vitality: this is to prepare the way for interest in the devotional, mental, and mystical yogas.

In the Orient itself there were several objectives combined in the physical level. Among them there was the intention to train the body to remain firm and steady during meditation. This promotes concentration of attention during the first stage, and helps to achieve mental stillness during the more advanced second stage. A further objective is to make the yogi the complete master of his body. If he succeeds, he is able to get a grip on himself and force the body into greater obedience to the higher self. Many mistake the means for the end and fail to see these higher objectives, or are trained (or train themselves) to carry the exercises to fantastic extremes. This is deplorable and is a waste of time and energy that could be given to the higher yogas. It is true that many, probably most, of the Oriental physical yogis, fakirs, and dervishes are victims of this error in the end. They miss the chance to rise to higher levels and fail to perceive that the life of the body is only a means of attaining a higher purpose which leads far beyond it. They lack sensitivity, subtlety, and intuition and thus write their names in the lists of spiritual failure. Perhaps the greatest danger of excessive attention to physical yoga is that it leads to identification with the physical body, just as excessive attention to devotional mysticism leads to identification with the emotions. In each case, the seekers stray away from the goal of the Quest subtly and unwittingly.

But such thoughts do not invalidate the virtue out of which they develop. The mastery of the body is a highly desirable virtue—not only on the so-called Spiritual Quest, but just as much in day-to-day living. That some of the postures used in the Oriental exercises are uncomfortable, others strange or dangerous, still others impossible to emulate by those who have lost their suppleness with advancing years is undoubtedly true and deplorable; but since I make no attempt to present the physical yoga system in its entirety here, nor even to copy any part of it blindly, there is no need to offer any excuses or to compose justifications. The practices, drills, regimes, purifications, and exercises described here are not wholly new, but some of the modifications are. In accord with the attitude I have learnt from philosophy, with its ideals of balance, co-ordination, practicality, and helpfulness, I follow in this book my habitual practice of selecting, adapting, altering, and then combining the ancient knowledge with modern scientific knowledge and combining what I have learnt in countries of the Orient outside India with both. The reader can walk with safety where otherwise he would need to proceed with caution.

It is not only the Indians who use physical methods for their psycho-spiritual systems. The ancient temple hierophants of the Nile Valley did so, too. Some of their exercises have been pictured on the walls of pharaonic tombs. The Coptic Christian occultists who succeeded them have inherited the secrets of some of the more dramatic and startling phenomena. Of such are Dr. Tahra Bey about whom I wrote in *A Search in Secret Egypt*, and also Hamid Bey, who was trained from the age of six to achieve complete bodily mastery. The dervishes of Arabia and Syria and other Mediterranean lands, who have mostly dispersed today, use such methods, too. Some of the exercises were devised to have a therapeutic value; others to achieve the glow of physical fitness. Granted that among these holy men there are men of different levels of understanding and different types of character; that a proportion are not at all holy, others mere beggars, and so on; the fact remains that there is the tradition of seeking out the God among them, so it would be a misconception to see only the surface value of the ancient systems of physical yoga.

A course of spiritual development which corrects the bad habits of the mind and purifies the feelings of the heart but shows no interest in the habits and conditions of the physical body is based on a one-sided concept of man. It is unbalanced. How can it yield any other than an unbalanced and incomplete result? Whether the body is ignored or considered, life must still be lived in its entirety by all human beings. This includes spiritually seeking human beings, and their bodies are still with them whatever they do or fail to do.

It is reasonable to suggest that we ought to understand something of the nature of the world in order to live in it more successfully and more harmoniously. The part of the world that is closest to us and most important for us is the body through which we experience it. To neglect that body or to ignore its needs is not necessarily a spiritual attitude. If it were, then there must have been an error in the Divine Creation! It has its own value, place, and purpose in the Divine World-Idea. They are high. At the present stage of human existence, there is no other way to durable spiritual development than through physical embodiments. The total sum of its varied experiences offer us the chance at first to learn and thus to progress, and later to overcome ourselves and thus to attain spiritual awareness. Through it the soul, sent by the World-Mind to gain experience and obtain growth, lives and functions in this world. Without it, how could the soul get the necessary range of experience to bring into manifestation its potential powers of thought, imagination, understanding, and decision at the lower level, and of ultimate consciousness at the higher level?

On this plane, the body is indeed the only medium of our existence and is not to be disconnected from our higher aspirations. A complete and competent spiritual instruction ought not to be so foolish as to neglect or overlook the physical frame of the disciple being instructed, but should see it with its several organs and higher senses as it truly is; that is, as an expression of Infinite Intelligence through which one can gather the experience needed to become fully aware of his relation to that Intelligence. There is another and usually much less considered point of view to this matter: the body contains countless little lives which look to us as their protector and leader and guide, which need and should get from us kindly attention. Knowledge of the laws which govern its sustenance, health, and functioning and which affect those lives is, therefore, a necessary step on the Quest and a necessary human duty. It is true that most people misuse the body through ignorance of these laws and injure it through succumbing to weakness of will. It is true that although it is only an instrument to be used for a certain higher purpose, they have perverted or ignored that purpose. It is true that they have indulged the body's senses and some of its organs to the extent of making this force and artificial indulgence the main object of living. Yet despite these errors it still remains a sacred temple of the Holy Ghost and the useful servitor of man's progression.

The physical body is neither an enemy to be harshly treated nor an encumbrance to be sadly denounced. When through the Quest's disciplines man establishes proper control of it, he will no longer regard it as an enemy of his spiritual aspirations, the paralysing weight on his spiritual being.

It was easy in earlier days to set up an opposition between body and soul when so little was known about the mind-body relationship. But in these days, when the influence and moral character of malfunctioning organs, nerve plexuses, and endocrine glands is scientifically better known, when psychosomatic medicine is tracing a connection between negative thoughts and physical sicknesses, the place of the flesh in the life of spiritual aspiration is better understood—although hardly better than it has been understood by the developed adepts of the ancient East and by a few seers of the modern West. This understanding reveals how susceptible the mind-force is, how the millions of tiny microorganisms which work together in a single community are the body. It is in truth and fact the Temple of the Spirit, a holy dwelling place wherein we are slowly learning lesson after lesson in the art of unfolding characteristics and awareness which bring us closer to our God-like Goal. How could philosophy fail to respect it?

It is a curious paradox which few of his commentators seem to have noted that although Jesus declared his Kingdom was not of this world he put so much time and effort into healing sickness and disease which are very much of this world. It is difficult to resolve this contradiction. If Jesus despised the body as he is often supposed to have done, why then did he trouble to heal it?

The religious, mental, and concentration-path yogis who regale their souls with sneers at the misguided physical yogis; the theologians who look suspiciously at the flesh, unsure whether it is the handiwork of God or Satan; and the metaphysicians who dismiss it altogether as not worth the attention which they give exclusively to abstract things are nevertheless unable to ignore the body when it falls sick. Whatever their opinion of it, they have then to take notice and take care of their physical tenement and get it treated. However much they despise the flesh they must still live in it. However much they argue the body away they must still use it. Behind every dismissive sentence directed against it there is a disquieting unbalance, an unhealthy refusal to face actuality which may draw on itself the punishment of malfunction, obstruction, and sickness. If it is such a handicap, why do they endure it at all? Why not discard it and live in the spirit world? Why waste time disciplining it when the simple act of committing suicide sets them free from its obstructive tactics?

Let us have a wiser balance! Why not sensibly and philosophically accept having a body, limited always and troublesome occasionally though it may be? Why, indeed, should any spiritual seekers feel guilty simply because they have a body? Their penance would be better directed toward their real sin—that they surrender *to* the ego instead of surrendering *the* ego. Even the most inveterate idealist must admit that physical surroundings influence the mind to some extent, that climate does affect temperament, that alcohol can bring about dramatic changes in a man's outlook, and that illness never exhilarates but often depresses the feelings. There is too close a relation between body and mind, too much interaction between them, to engage safely in any enterprise which proposes to reconstruct the mind and yet totally ignores the body. To be the master of oneself is to be the master of the body—one's instrument—as well as of the mind. And if the goal is both mental and physical, as it has to be if we are to live in the world of physical acts, a solely mental technique cannot be enough; a physical one needs to be added to complete it. But by getting the body under control, we shall find it easier to get the mind under control. There are physical aids with the general aim of self-mastery which may profitably be used, just as there are physical hindrances which make the Quest harder.

Since the philosophical attainment of illumination is primarily a mental affair, the means to attain it are primarily mental also. That is why so prominent a place has been given in all traditions to mental exercises, devotional attitudes, and emotional disciplines. But because man has to live in and use his physical body, and especially because there is some influence of the body upon the mind, part of this means must necessarily be physical. The Quest has to be staged progressively, like all journeys. It begins with the body, which must be clean, disciplined, and controlled. Philosophy cannot be dissociated from a proper use of the physical organism. Why should it stop short with a proper use of the emotional nature or of the intellectual nature alone? The ancient Greeks' respect for the body, their cultivation of its vitality and beauty, can be joined to the ancient Hindus' fight against its desires and appetites. The ideals of the Greek masters were not incompatible with those of the Indian ones. Both the athlete and sculptor of Greece and the hatha yogi of India desired physical perfection, although their ways to it were so different.

The cleansing process is simply one to remove the obstacles and push back the limitations on the seeker's spiritual journey. It has to be brought into all departments of his activity—his actions, his intentions, his words, his thoughts, and his feelings—and along with them all, into his body. The latter will correct its instincts which can then, whereas only brokenly and distortedly before, bring him information that is valuable for keeping the body as a pure temple of the Spirit. But artificial modes of living either pervert them so completely that the bad is taken for good until the body breaks down, or else repress these instincts so effectually that the ego gets more and more confused until the nerves break down. The body must be cleansed and refined at some stage of the Quest. If this is not done at the beginning, it will have to be done during the middle stages. If the reformation of life, character, and consciousness begins with the body, it will have to include the mind later. If it begins with the mind, it will have to include the body later—for the latter's influence on the mind will prove inescapable and will have to be brought into harmony with the Quest's ideal. Its pressure upon the mind in many cases is as powerful as the environment's pressure upon the body. The artist seeking to create beauty, the thinker seeking to discover truth, and the mystic seeking to feel intuition are subject to this pressure during the earlier stages of their endeavours. They free themselves from it only when they can reach the deep, rapt absorption of the later stages. This cleansing of the body, the emotions, and the mind is an indispensable preparatory stage of the Quest. For the advanced techniques, it is a necessary means of clearing the way for the influx of spiritual forces during meditation. Meditation which is not accompanied by purification leads easily to pseudo-intuitions. The aspirant may follow at one and the same time the paths of purification and meditation, or he may place them in their logical order and attend to them consecutively. There is much to be said for both choices, although tradition has usually said that purification should precede meditation.

The food taken into the body, the emotions taken into the heart, and the thoughts taken into the mind must be carefully screened as part of the disciplinary regime in the earlier and preparatory stages of the Quest. This will protect against the misdirection of the life-giving forces which will be aroused and brought into them by the Quest's practices. It will enable seekers to receive without instruction the Light of the Overself and to reflect it in their activities. It will restore a truer health to them. The lower nature will no longer be able to prevent them from becoming aware of their higher nature.

The Western metaphysician or Indian yogi who is uninterested in the question of health merely because it concerns the condition of the despised body or of the unreal ego is unbalanced. The body has been formed ultimately out of the Divine Substance, out of the same light waves from which the entire universe has been formed. How then can we call it evil? No, what is evil is the body's rulership over the mind without regard for the higher purposes for which we temporarily live in the body. Balance must be established between the needs of the body and the functioning of the inner life. If we undervalue the body and treat it as nothing, then we take risks with its welfare and set up obstructions to our illumination. The body is an expression of the World-Mind and it is our duty to love and care for it in the right way and give the proper attention to its various needs. We must value health and realize the importance of the body's influence upon the emotions and intellect. In the highest Oriental philosophy—usually given only to the few—balance is allotted an important place. The philosopher will attend to the necessities of his bodily existence as carefully as to his spiritual existence.

It is not too difficult to get some sort of spiritual feeling, peace, or awareness by simple means, especially by fervent prayer or intense aspiration. The annals of religious experience, conversion, and monasticism testify to that. But to get a fuller and deeper awareness, correct in its result and durable in its nature, is comparatively much harder and more demanding. The effort and practices required are more complex since the mind must be trained, emotions cleansed, and the body disciplined, for they all affect each other and obstruct or help the attainment of the desirable result. Those who are not satisfied with less must be ready to pay the higher price than those who are. This is the reason why the way of spiritual self-discovery introduces physical exercises and techniques not commonly associated with religious seeking in the Western world. This is why anyone who is dissatisfied with the life of mere impulse and irrational habit and who wishes to bring it under his own control will have to practise exercises in some form. Now, exercise means accompanying discipline, restraint, and the discomfort of change, all of which involve self-control. The saving power of this teaching is proportionate to, and dependent on, the self-control achieved by its followers.

It was an ancient Chinese sage, Lao Tzu, who said that those who conquered other men showed power but those who conquered themselves showed strength. On this Quest it is needful to calculate strength of will. The aspirant needs it to practise self-control, to overcome harmful desires, and to reject negative thoughts. He needs it to gain control of his actions which result from those desires and thoughts. Only so can he obtain full victory over the animal part of his nature.

The body is to be his servant, a willing and obedient servant. But it can carry out his bidding properly only if it is trained to do so, and easily only if it is strong and healthy. A sick and diseased body is less able to obey the disciplining will and reasoning mind than a healthy one. It becomes a gaol when it ought to be a temple. So far as right living will bring it to better condition, the aspirant who is strong enough and receptive enough will put himself willingly under the needed discipline to ensure those habits.

All through history, spiritual guides and religious prophets, ethical teachers and enrapt mystics have told humanity to elevate ideals, conduct, thought; to discipline self, passion, emotion; but they have seldom told humanity what practical procedure to adopt to make such drastic changes possible. How many good persons have found themselves in the disquieting position of Saint Paul when the melancholy confession was wrung from him: "For the good that I would, I do not; but the evil which I would not, that I do!" What is the use of urging them to live up to high ideals if they lack the means whereby this can be done? If a man is told to be good, he is given counsel that may yet be worthless to him. If he is taught the Law of Recompense and told why it will profit him to be good, the counsel may appeal (should he be a reasonable man) but he may still lack the strength of will to implement it; he needs to be taught *how* to be good. The purification of the body is the first step in this direction.

Anyone who takes philosophy seriously enough will have to take to its discipline. This will assault his formed habits just as much as its psychology will assault his self-conceit. His way of living—his diet, sleep, and rest, for instance—will have to be examined and where necessary reformed. A real Truth-seeker is not only willing to search for and try out new ways but is actually eager to do so. The story of his regime is one of the dynamic reaching for the new, the untried.

Too many have been kept away from these ideas of reform because they have been associated with monomaniacs and eccentrics, with foolish diets and indiscriminate propaganda. Indeed, the Quester will need to keep these new habits to himself—for society, mesmerized by so many faults and timid conventions as it is, may ostracize him as an odd and peculiar person. Society's attitude is understandable and even pardonable; but why should a fellow Quester who does not care to adopt these habits or who rejects their value be intolerant of them? If an ideal or practice is believed by any other school of thought than the one which he happens to be following as being good in its time and just as right for its place, he ought not to belittle it. Why can he not simply turn aside and leave it to those who think they need it? He ought to recognize their perfect right to follow a different way of thought, even if it seems to him an inferior way.

The average person is disinclined to practise any technical method of self-discipline. Why should he voluntarily suffer a dislocation of his settled character, habit, or routine which it involves? Why should he trouble to accept a bothersome or austere regime when he can more easily do without it? Why should he put himself in training with special exercises if he is quite unfettered by any obligation to do so? Why, in short, enforce hard labours or harsh curbs which society does not ask from him and which natural inclination resists? Alas, it is easier to get such a man to spend his money foolishly; he will work apathetically at self-possession.

It is needful to make the reminder that all these suggestions apply only to those who have definitely committed themselves to the Quest and not to those who accept the Truth but wish only to read and think about it, or to those who merely wish to acquire information about it, much less to those who are not at all concerned with it in any way whosoever. It is indeed essential to understand that the restrictions and disciplines laid down here are not intended for ordinary persons with ordinary aims. The practices are for the use of a certain class of reader only. They have special ends in view and are often only temporary means to those ends: when their fulfilment is secured, some of them may be dropped if desired, or kept up if the habit has become attractive. It is by the light of this particular intention that the instructions given should be read. This class is a comparatively small one and those who do not feel the call to join its limited number are under no necessity at all to adopt the hard trainings described here. The worldling who is eager to make his life as comfortable and as easy as possible, as well as the self-indulgent weakling who seeks to cram it with pleasure, will not welcome such regimes.

The Quester who is not hard with himself and not willing to reform his habits will not go so far or so quickly as the one who is both. Great yearnings for a better state are not enough; he must do something to gain it. When he first reads about these disciplines he may quite likely feel alarm, and as he continues to read he may even feel despair. Such severe austerities are not for us in the world, he thinks, but only for those in the cloister or the cave. Yet if he regards the regimes as inhumanly hard, what is there in them which is not comprised in the admonitions of Jesus and in the repeated counsel of the apostle Paul to rule the flesh? The answer to those who can go along with the rightness of the theory but must stop before the difficulty of applying it is that the body is teachable. Physical habits are not set for all eternity but are amenable to a sort. The difficulty of these objectors in moving from the will to do what is right to the act itself resolves itself under the proper training.

If even such disciplining of the body, hardening of the will, and control-ling of the emotions as Philosophy enjoins seem too stoical to be worth enduring, the question may be asked: Is it not more prudent, in an era which has shown up the wickedness and weakness of man on so wide a scale, to develop strength little by little now, than to remain too un-prepared and too weak to be able to react well enough to the times ahead for the human race—which seem to demand much greater strength from it than it shows today? Finally, it can only be said that people who have lost their way have to be taught the laws of higher living anew. Whoever willingly practises these teachings and works faithfully at these exercises will find that the body tends to become more and more the trained instrument of his will and purpose. As he grows in moral stature and psycho-physical balance, he will come to see as the Stoics saw that the compensation for all his disciplinary labour and self-denial is in the virtue and cleanness themselves. They will give him sufficient satisfaction and confer a happiness of their own.

When not only the prohibited actions themselves are no longer indul-ged in, but even the very thought of them is always absent, when they no longer appear attractive to the desire nature, then he may regard himself as having achieved this purification. If the entire program is fully carried out with an implacable ardour in the pursuit of such self-mastery, he will become a re-born man.

Some people may misunderstand these recommendations to physical self-reform as an espousal of joyless asceticism. This will dishearten or even frighten them, for few persons in these days can find either the requisite external circumstances or the requisite internal aspiration to adopt the regimes so often associated with austere monastic life. The admiration of asceticism for which the ancient and medieval world was famous is not shared by the modern world. It finds few eager followers today. Its pallid figures are not attractive.

Like all things, asceticism has its use which is to be admired and its abuse which is to be reprehended. Its history shows much unfortunate confusion of values. It has not only run to extremely exaggerated forms but also to wildly perverted ones. It has in the past been extremely widespread in the Orient, so much that if anyone there seeks to take up the pursuit of Spiritual Truth seriously he is told that he must become a completely inhibited ascetic—leaving the world, not drinking, not smoking, not eating meat, not marrying, or leaving his wife if he is already married. To a lesser extent, there were the same restrictions in medieval Christian Europe.

The balanced life of Philosophy does not run to these extremes. It does not consider physical pleasure and aesthetic enjoyment as evils to be ruthlessly eliminated. It accepts them but disciplines them and trains the impulse toward them. They are kept in the place where they belong and not allowed to interfere with the higher purposes of life. Comfortable surroundings and the artistic presentation of meals, for instance, may be indulged in as part of the human pursuit of happiness so long and so far as they do not weaken the resolute search for moral perfection and spiritual awareness. The ascetic who thinks good clothes and modern sanitation, for instance, are going to deprive him of spirituality had certainly better do without these things. The philosophical student, however, has no such fear because he has a somewhat different view of what constitutes spirituality: for him it is primarily a matter of the mind. He does not see any spiritual crime in demanding proper clothing, good food, and some of the useful amenities of material resources and modern invention. He sees no sin against the Holy Ghost in sharing the lonely caravanserai of life with a wife and then with a child or two if he feels such needs strongly enough.

The elderly, bearded abbot of an Indian monastery where I stayed for a while told me that as a young man he had crossed the country to live in the lower slopes of the Himalayas and devote himself to meditation. But he was unused to the freezing cold and misty dampness of the cave which he inhabited. After eighteen months, he developed such acute rheumatism that he was unable to meditate at all and had to abandon his enterprise and return to the warmer plains, where, he discovered in the end, he could master meditation and become an adept at it. The abbé Vianney, famous throughout France in the early nineteenth century as an ascetic holy priest, deliberately slept on bare damp boards to mortify himself and increase his holiness. He contracted severe neuralgia and suffered its torments for fifteen years. We may well ask, was such an extreme measure really necessary? Could he not have achieved his undoubted holiness just as well without it?

Admittedly, asceticism has a part to play in everyone's passage through earthly life and especially in the aspirant's. If he takes monastic vows, he is put under discipline; if he remains in the world, he must put himself under discipline, otherwise there would be no difference between the world's values and his own spiritual values. But asceticism is only a part of the means to his goal: it ought not to be made the complete goal in his life as it has indeed been made in those mystical circles where people have come to value it for its own sake alone. The discipline it provides should be sane, limited, and controlled; nor should it necessarily be confined to the monastic form only. We have to learn self-discipline and self-control, but these are qualities which today are not less learned in the world than out of it.

The paramount factor of mysticism is essentially the mental and not the physical one. Renunciation is a new attitude of mind, not a new set of monkish robes. All the maturer mystics have come in time to see and to proclaim this irrefutable truth. The others who overrate external mysticism imperil their position, for where the giving up of outward satisfactions is wholly unnatural and wholly false there is certain to be an eventual reaction. When that happens the renunciation will itself be renounced, so that the effort and time put into it are wasted. In fact, the first words of the first sermon Buddha ever preached were addressed to five monks whom he warned against exaggerating the value of their asceticism!

There are valuable features in asceticism of which Philosophy gladly makes use. There is a time in most aspirants' lives when they must let its cool waves flow over them. So far-reaching a change of living habits must logically have equally far-reaching results. It does. They go all through the physical body, which is obvious, and also all through the emotional and passional natures, which is not quite so obvious. The ascetic regime was considered a necessity in ancient times in the study of philosophy, for it helped externally to give the calmness, leisure, concentration, and perseverance needed for the study. It was an effort to shake off bad emotional entanglements, exaggerated egoistic possessiveness, and degrading bodily enslavements. Such an effort cannot be other than commendable. It was an attempt to bring passions into subjection to reason and to will.

Disciplines of the body conducted within reasonable limits and for limited periods are excellent. Philosophy puts them in their place, does not exaggerate them, and does not abandon its balance for them. They prepare the way for the elementary experiences and initiatory adventures of the Quest. But when excessive significance is attached to them, or when they are carried out with exaggerated fanaticism, they begin to do harm as well as good. The mind's balance is then upset. Indeed, the difference between a reasonable and moderate discipline, such as is advocated here, and extreme ascetic austerity, such as some have traditionally practised, is sometimes the difference between sanity and madness.

No ascetic discipline need be carried to an unnecessary extreme, nor further than its proper intention—which is to give physical self-control. The aspirant is not called on to forgo some things and abstain from others merely because it is traditional in asceticism to do so, for he may reject a number of those traditions as unnecessarily self-martyring. If he is called upon for any of these abstentions in Philosophy, it is because they give strength to his will, protection to his meditations, purity and fitness to his body. He is not asked to bear a cross of suffering in anguish but to carry a staff of support in joy! The fanatics and extremists have made asceticism at once their strength and their weakness. The philosophers have made it a useful instrument for their perfectly balanced manifold purposes.

There is another side of asceticism whose original intention of reducing worldly entanglements to a minimum is excellent, but whose common degeneration is not. That intention served to curb the desire for luxury at some point, and to simplify the life at another point. Modern existence is too often cluttered with too many material possessions. These demand care and attention, time and energy, thought and feeling, which the average Quester is rarely able to find enough of to provide for study, reflection, and meditation anyway. Somewhere he will probably have to sacrifice something if he is to gain them for his spiritual need. A time usually comes when he finds it desirable to reorganize his way of life so as not to be encumbered by so many things. It may not be easy and it will not be pleasant to strip himself of many unessential objects. Yet if he trains himself to demand less physical luxury and fewer physical gadgets, this will put him in a better position to get control of his desires, strengthen his will, and so to master himself. Even those who are unwilling to go so far and who are unattracted by the prospect of a simpler life must recognize the legitimacy of this attitude. A rigidly ascetic vow of poverty is not only unnecessary but also for most of us impracticable. The Indian yogi can successfully beg his way across his country; the tropic dweller can manage to exist on very few necessities; but the Euramerican can hardly be expected to do the same. If he were to give away all possessions without at the same time getting into a monastery, he would find outward trouble and not inner peace. To have this he must have some money. But, by simplifying his way of life and reducing his social ambitions, he need not strive so hard to get the money he *really* needs.

Yet even this worthy objective has been turned too often by foolish ascetics into a worship of unnecessary squalor, discomfort, and torment; into a rejection of beautiful things and a repudiation of art; into a high valuation of drab and uncomfortable things, as well as into a deliberate repression of the finer aesthetic feelings. How foolish their attitude is can be judged by the methods given in my book *The Quest of the Overself* for using those very feelings as valuable helps in mastering the art of meditation.

The proper intention of mortifying the lust of luxury is to keep a man from getting too much involved in earthly things. It is an arguable point as to where luxury begins, for obviously the line will rise higher as one's station in life or professional circumstances rises higher. It is arguable, too, how far the fine surroundings and beautiful objects are necessities or luxuries. Asceticism has often set itself flatly against these things. Yet if the Quest leads to the very spirit of beauty itself, why should one of the means adopted to that end be the joyless, puritanical denial of all beautiful expressions and a deliberate cultivation of ugly ones? A simpler life, avoiding the perils which accompany ambition, avarice, or luxury, may be desirable; but a severer one, holding in contempt things which are valuable for human refinement and well-being, is not. To give a part of one's life to a sane, restricted discipline is good and strengthening, but to give the whole of it to bleak denial and utter negation is bad and unbalancing.

In earlier writings, I made some criticism of the concept of an antinomy between body and soul and of the fanatical, self-tormenting type of asceticism which espoused it. The real objection was to the metaphysical error which failed to see that the flesh is the temple of the Spirit and that the body is to be studied and respected as such. The extremists sought to punish the flesh masochistically and often uselessly. Moreover, they fell into a sort of spiritual pride far too easily and exalted themselves far above those who did not think as they did.

A sane and balanced asceticism, on the contrary, should seek to make the body clean, purified, disciplined, and obedient to the highest dictates of intuition, reason, and will. It should consider the body also as a symbol of the entire universe, reflecting in design and operation the same Infinite Intelligence there discernible. Such an asceticism is worthy of the highest regard.

If for years I opposed the extreme forms taken by asceticism and pleaded for milder forms, another of the reasons why I did this is because so few people have the capacity to adopt them. But, through being shown a livable, attainable way for modern times, many people who would otherwise have shrunk in dismay from applying the spiritual teaching they read about actually became aspirants. In this way, many were brought into the study who would not have touched it otherwise. I tried to make the Quest a little easier than I found it—less formidable to the eyes and more suited to the capacities of modern men and women.

I must repeat the warning that those chapters which deal with the physical regimes, yoga exercises, and disciplines ought not to get undue and disproportionate attention, for they represent an elementary and not an advanced outlook. They are intended to help beginners who usually find it difficult, first, to understand the metaphysical teachings; second, to practise the mystical exercises; third, to adopt the attitude of seeking God or the Overself above all other things; and fourth, to abandon their identification with the personal consciousness. They cannot jump into the advanced ideas or practices but must develop by slow degrees. These physical methods are a help to such earlier development; but, in the end, if the beginner is to advance at all, he will have to rise to the study of the metaphysics of Truth and to the practice of the exercises in mystical meditation. For only so can he outgrow the universal human conception of our selves. Only so can he rise out of the widespread mesmerism of this world and the illusion of this body into actual realization of Jesus's statement, "I and My Father are One," meaning that there is only One Infinite and Eternal Reality, Life, Power, and Mind, that This alone is all there really is, and that there are not even two Powers—Reality and illusion—for Reality exists alone as unsullied, undivided, and unpersonalized Consciousness.

From that exalted height, all these physical regimes and purificatory austerities assume an insignificant importance and the intuitive feeling and rational understanding of Consciousness, Reality, and Self an immense one.

2

THE BODY

Buddha ascetically turned in disgust from the human body. He could see it only as an assemblage of loathsome elements. Plato artistically turned towards it in joy. He received inspiration through its beauty. Neither Indian nor Greek was quite right nor quite wrong. Each deliberately unveiled only a part of the picture. Whoever wishes to see the whole picture must put together both the bright top part and the dark lower part. He must comprehend that the body is doomed to decay and die but that its informing life is destined to grow into grandeur. Thus the finite form becomes a portal to the infinite reality.

2

The body is not to be despised with the ascetic nor neglected with the mystic. It is to be understood and rightly used. It is to be cared for as one of the instruments whose total contribution will enable us to fulfil the spiritual purpose of life on earth.

3

We use our minds and our bodies badly. And we do this through ignorance, through the lack of instruction on their proper use. The right use of the body and the correct provision of its needs are arts to be learned. The civilized man is not born with them. He is the unfortunate hereditary victim of generations of faulty modern habits. There is a better way to use the bodily mechanism than the habitual one of most Westerners. Philosophy, knowing the mind-body relationship, is just as applicable to such apparently simple and trivial—but hygienically and psychologically important—matters as our use of this mechanism in sitting, walking, standing, breathing, and even bending. It prescribes wise rules for living, eating, and drinking.

4

Knowing the laws of mental and physical hygiene and obeying them will make him a better student of truth than will being ignorant of them.

5

How many who recognize truth when it deals with metaphysical and mystical subjects, cannot recognize it when it deals with physical regimes! If we ask why this should be so, the answer is to be sought in the power of prevalent custom and inherited habit.

6

The body's presence and activity, importance and influence, its demands for health and strength and care, can be ignored in his experience only for a short time. Sooner or later he must turn to notice them, and if he seeks meaning, to account for them.

7

We need the body—all of us, not materialists nor ordinary persons only—therefore we must respect it. It is with the ears that we listen to Beethoven: that is, with the body. It is with the eyes that we read beautiful poetry: again with the body. Let us not decry the body.

8

If enlightenment is to be full, and completely balanced, it must not only occur in the thinking intellect and emotional feeling; it must also occur in the acting physical body.

9

The physical body is each person's responsibility. He has to live with it as well as live in it. The failure to care properly for it makes it complain. The only language in which it can do so with most men and women is that of sickness, disease, or malfunction; with others, a silent intuitive feeling is enough. But in the first case although its speech is heard, its message is often misunderstood, ignored, or rejected.

10

He can and may transcend the body and the body's world or deny them in mystical meditation, metaphysical speculation. But this does not get rid of them. They are a fact which confronts him as soon as the speculation passes, or the meditation ebbs. It is then that the value of health must be recognized, the conditioning by surroundings properly appraised.

11

Only on such a physical foundation can the mental exercises have enough good results; otherwise it is too hard a struggle to aspire and try to meditate. The modern civilized environment is artificial, is hostile to spiritual development, and periodic retreat or flight from it is essential.

12

Those who feel they are making no progress at all and those who find what little they do make is slow and tedious, should look to neglected factors in their individual case. The physical body, for instance: does it get right diet, exercise, breathing, and relaxing, or does it sin against the laws of hygienic living?

13

Sane and balanced life commands us to keep physically fit so far as doing so is within our power—which means so far as karma permits. Physical fitness is the harmonious and efficient functioning of each part of the body. The yoga of body control must be broadly interpreted to mean not postural exercises alone, but the discipline of the whole physical organism. It is better for instance, to eat brown bread than to be able to contort the body in yoga posture number 57!

14

Not only mind, not only heart, but also body is the chamber in which a master must work.

15

Although he taught men to give up the world and its ways, although he persuaded whoever would respond to adopt the inner life as a full-time occupation, Buddha was balanced enough to declare that a healthy body was a great benefit to everyone. Although he rejected the unnecessary, the greedy, or the imprudent gratification of the body's desires and appetites, he commended the satisfaction of its essential needs. Although he taught a strict discipline of the body, he did not teach men to despise it. His praise of good health showed his wisdom.

16

We have to live with the body for the rest of our lives, and therefore must accommodate it in this quest. It is not to be denounced as a tomb if, by careful and pure living, it can be turned into a temple. It must be ruled, disciplined, used as an instrument. It needs to learn to sit still without fidgets when we wish it to do so for meditation periods. It needs to learn to like pure natural foods. Its lusts must be dealt with and mastered, not accepted feebly.

17

Everyone who wants to reject these purifying disciplines of habit and progressive reforms of regime is perfectly entitled to do so, and on any grounds that appeal to him. But he ought to do so modestly and quietly and humbly for, as personal hygienes, they represent the tested ideas and practices of thousands of years of experience among thousands of mystics, holy men, saints, and sages, and in continents far apart from one another.

18

We are spiritually saved only when the whole of our being is cleansed and renewed, when body, mind, and feeling are purified and reborn. It is not enough to cleanse the moral character only.

19

Most students know that the preparatory work includes purifying the heart of base feelings and clearing the mind of negative thoughts—arduous but necessary work. Few students know that it also includes cleansing the body of toxic matter.

20

The body is to be brought under his command, made accustomed to do his higher will, that which serves his best self, his purer consciousness.

21

There is a wise use of the body and an unwise one. The philosopher increases its value as a servant by improving its health and increasing its vital force. These energies will be used to strengthen concentration and sustain meditation on one side of his being, and to cultivate will and rule the passions on the other. The unwise way is to drive the body into fanatic asceticisms and foolish extremes. It should become a useful ally.

22

Regeneration of the inner being must be begun or completed by attention to the outer being—the body. Those who are so captivated by the inner work that they fail to see the importance of the other, make a mistake.

23

The faulty use of the body is a consequence of the failure to bring both awareness and reflection into it. This is to be guarded against because civilized living has substituted artificial habits for the natural ones of the savage. The bad results of this failing make their appearance most often after the age of fifty.

24

The man who starts to seek for God with little more than his earnestness or eagerness, has not started with enough. He needs also a cleaner body and a clearer mind.

25

To deny any organ of the body its legitimate function is to deny harmony, coordination, total well-being to the body.

26

They have forced habits, foods, and environments on the body which it not only would never have freely chosen for itself but would instantly have rejected if given the chance to be heard.

27

The human being who tries to ignore his physical conditions, and especially his physical body, does not in the end usually succeed in doing so. This is true in the West and to a lesser degree in the East. If cancer makes its appearance in that body, as a result of his karma—which it mostly is—he is compelled to reckon with it.

28

This thing, this fleshly body, which ascetics have hated and saints have despised, is a holy temple. The divine Life-force is always latently present in it and, aroused, can sweep through every cell, making it sacred.

29

If the Word was made flesh, if the Cosmic Mind manifested this vast universe out of its own substance, if the world is divine, why should we be stopped from enjoying our life in it?

30

The body in itself is not evil, could not be if it expresses divine intelligence. Life in it is an inevitable phase of the entity's development; the experiences garnered from it lead to lessons learned and truths understood.

31

The mystic who recognizes the never-ceasing wonder and divine worth of his body, who accepts it as the stage on and through which he has to fulfil himself and realize his ideal, is not degrading that ideal or falling back into bondage but is actually carrying out the high purpose which is held before man in the cosmic scheme.

32

Every part of the body shows forth this infinite wisdom.

33

The body gives us our existence in this time-spaced world but its service does not stop there; for, its flesh cleansed and its breathing quieted, it lends itself to higher purpose—no less than acting as a temple of the holy Spirit for blissful meditation.

34

Philosophic asceticism practises disciplines because it properly values the body, not because it hates the body. Incarnation is an opportunity for salvation. The body is a holy temple. The flesh is a revelation of the World-Mind's working.

35

The early Church Father Tertullian made a good point (albeit for a bad superstition) that if man had been made in the image of God it was so in his whole person, and it was a ridiculous stand to denounce the flesh as worthless. Irenaeus and Justin took the same stand (for the same bad reason) and even proclaimed that spirit was interblent with flesh.

36

How close is his relationship to that other Self, that godlike Overself! And not only his mind's relationship but also his body's. For in the centre of every cell in blood, marrow, flesh, and bone, there is the void that holds, and is, pure Spirit.

37

This physical life may seem like death to the inner life; yet it is our only means of developing the inner life.

38

All these physical methods are only preliminary, are only disciplines to establish the proper bodily conditions for inner work. They can not of themselves bring about spiritual illumination.

39

The body is our physical home. Through its five senses we may suffer pain and misery or enjoy satisfaction and pleasure. Therefore it should be well treated and well cared for, kept healthy as far as we can. This is not only a personal need but also a spiritual duty for its condition may obstruct or assist the inner work.

40

The earth is the scene where man is placed to achieve his spiritual development. The body is the only direct contact he has with it: How foolish is it to mistreat the body through ignorance, abuse it through carelessness, or neglect it through laziness?

41

The belief that any physical method can liberate man spiritually or evolve him mystically is shallow and deceptive. But if it cannot fulfil these aims it can indirectly promote them by providing more favourable conditions for their attainment.

42

That this way of purer living leads to a higher vitality, a greater physical buoyancy than he would otherwise have had is a pleasant incidental result. But the deeper result, which most concerns aspirants, is a more active intuitive life and a less active animal nature.

43

If we will take sufficient care of the body and give sufficient thought to its experiences, if we will follow the counsel of reason rather than the impulse of appetite, its health will be fostered, its life prolonged, and its functioning improved.

44

If we treat the body carefully and heed the laws of health, we will have fewer obstacles in the way of spiritual efforts. Food is important for this purpose. Tensions in the muscles should be avoided, for there is an influence on the mind from the body.

45

The body (like the soul) gives messages of counsel, warning, or approval to him but too often he does not listen to them, does not understand them, or does not want his complacency (formed by tendencies, habits, and surroundings) disturbed.

46

The animal inheritance—the body's instincts, appetites, and passions— must be controlled and disciplined if these higher interests are to bear any fruit. Time, strength, attention, food, sex, activity and nonactivity, sleep and waking must all be regulated.

47

The hindrances which wrong bodily regimes put in his Quest are not only physical but also psychic emotional and mental.

48

The condition of a man's health, the medical state of his body, may contribute to his spiritual outlook, may enfeeble or enliven his faith.

49

If union with the Overself-consciousness is to be achieved, or progress to that goal made, the body ought also to share in the benefits received. It too ought to be freer from discordant elements, organs, or operations.

50

The wise student will recognize that he gains more than he loses by such sacrifices as this discipline of the body calls for. The benefits of resisting custom's dominance are both disproportionate and durable, with a value so high as to make the discipline bearable and the sacrifices smaller.

51

When he hears about these ascetic-sounding regimes a chill sets in. But what is it that rebels against them? It is the ego, the weakness of human will. Yet the rebellion is ill-founded, for the body is not tortured by being brought under control—only its perverted, exaggerated, or enslaving appetites suffer by doing so. The regimes themselves are sensible and are not fantastic fads. They are simply indications of the quester's need to live more carefully than other people, and to change habits which are bad. They are hygienic recommendations offered to those who want to advance their spiritual journey more quickly.

52

The bodily cells are so pervaded with toxic materials, so clogged with them, so contaminated by them, that this purificatory work is an essential preliminary to the mystical work, proper for most aspirants except those who have the inborn capability of quickly rising to an intense concentration which frees the cells from such poisons.

53

There is a mass of improperly digested, half-decayed food material lying in the intestines in a fermenting condition, while farther on there are accumulated deposits of petrified impurities on the lining of the colon and the membrane of the bowels. These substances are rejected by the body, which suffers by their presence but is unable to free itself from them without conscious and willing co-operation on the part of its owner. The body's physiological processes are clogged and encumbered by them and its nervous system and brain organ polluted by the inferior blood brought to nourish them.

54

To achieve this aim, a certain preparation as well as purification of the body is required. The spine must be cleared of adhesions, congestions, distortions, shrinkings, and nerve branch pressures. The tissues and blood have to be cleansed of the toxic materials accumulated in them.

55

That salvation which frees a man from enslavement to his lower nature is necessary and good, but it goes only part of the way to fulfilling his needs. His fleshly body also requires salvation. It ought to be freed from its poisoned, clogged, and unnatural condition.

56

The body cannot respond so freely to the subtle forces if it is saturated with destructive acids or clogged with decaying material, nor can the brain and nervous system respond so freely if they are stupefied by alcohol or drugs.

57

As the consciousness evolves to a higher level, so the body it functions through must become more refined in quality and purified in nature.

58

Mental equilibrium, yoga, cannot be attained without changing the habits which obstruct it. Even if the requisite purification of the body's cells and blood from all toxins has been achieved, a man must still refrain from starting on those ways which caused toxemia.

59

There is a common error that drugs and medicines are enough to keep us in good health. They are not. The only things that can do so are correct living habits, right thinking habits, and proper eating habits. A knowledge of personal hygiene will keep us in better health than a hundred boxes of pills.

60

We must learn to conform to the laws of hygienic living—mental and physical—if we want to achieve a sound mind in a sound body. We may not break those laws with impunity, nor believe that because we have been spiritually healed once we are exempt from them always.

61

The desire to gain purity must provide the power to follow the regimes needed for it. The sediment of egotism in the mind and animality in the flesh cannot be cleared out unless this desire grows strong and remains enduring.

62

The mental courage to cast out those wrong habits of living which ignorance of spiritual hygiene has allowed him to pick up, must show itself.

63

It is unwise and unfair to expect the beneficial result of such changes in living habit to manifest themselves at once. Yet in a number of cases this is what they do; in most others the disagreeable eliminative symptoms manifest first.

64

The body of the illumined man is subject to the same laws as the body of the unillumined one. Any violation of those laws through ignorance or custom may lead to sickness in both men. Each will of course react differently to the suffering caused by the sickness. But knowledge of higher laws does not exempt the illuminate from learning and obeying the lower ones.

65

The work of purifying the physical organism will be completed in time only to give way to the work of regenerating it. But this second task can only be undertaken if the necessary knowledge is available, which is not ordinarily the case.

66

What he is emotionally and mentally expresses itself to some extent in his body, in his face and even in the way he holds his body and carries himself, and still more remarkably in the very movements he makes. Some pioneer work in this research was done by Westerners such as F. Messias Alexander, Dr. Mensendieck, and Gaston Mengel. In the East, Japanese Zen masters developed this theme several centuries ago.

67

Because of the closeness between body and mind, whatever is experienced in one is reflected in the other. The Japanese masters understand this and detect from the physical positions taken by the body in its movements something of the condition within himself. We ourselves know that there is a connection between the pace and manner of breathing and the emotional condition. We can see how mental tension is reflected in muscular tension of the body; thus it is useful to learn about these different conditions and to benefit by the good ones and avoid the bad ones.

68

How often does a man's mental condition depend on his physical needs, on whether he has had too little or too much sleep or food, on whether he is exposed to tropical heat or arctic cold!

69

Ownership of a physical form lays a certain responsibility upon him. To evade this, in the name of metaphysical truth, may lead to an intellectually deceptive freedom from it but cannot lead to a factually physical freedom from the effects of his neglect.

70

The metaphysicians or mystics, particularly the Indian ones, who speak slightingly of the body and deny that it is the self, would conform more to the realities of experience if they said that it is a *part* of the self.

71

The further answer to those who preach neglect of the body is to point out how limited would be their life, and hence their consciousness, if they lost a bodily part such as a hand, or a bodily sense such as taste. Instead of giving the fullest freedom of expression to the divine life-power within themselves, they would give it no more than a partial expression.

72

The body is there; it has existence, life, and above all, inescapable needs. Let it not be despised, for we must use its services. But let it not conquer us and stifle our aspirations.

73

He is trapped in the nerve structure, the glands, and the brain cells of his physical body, dependent upon them and conditioned by them. To ignore the body in his spiritual seeking is foolish unpardonable neglect, but to deny it altogether, as some cults do, is simply absurd.

74

The body must not be ignored, for consciousness, even will, is inter-woven with it, affected by it while moods are born, or at least related, to it.

75

Whether he is a high mystic or an ordinary man, he is saddled with a body which must be cared for, nourished and cleaned, kept alive. This is to say that it demands attention, thought, a portion of consciousness. Any attempt to decry it on the Vedantic ground of unreality is absurd. Every illness mocks such foolishness.

76

I can not forget the shock I experienced when on three different occasions and in three different parts of the world I heard a spiritual teacher whom I admired and respected and who had a substantial follow-ing, express complete indifference to the condition of the body. One was a European, the other two were Oriental. They expressed it not merely as a personal opinion, but also as a part of their teaching, for their disciples were present on each occasion. One of the Orientals fell ill within a few weeks and had to cancel his meetings until he recovered. The other died under painful circumstances, that is, from a most painful disease. The European was struck down within a few years and had to undergo a major operation from which he recovered, but with all his vitality gone, his creativity at an end, and personal work practically finished. I asked myself, "Were the Gods trying to correct the attitude of these three spiritual guides? Can we afford to ignore the question of the health and sickness of the body? Is it not a fact that sickness destroys our pleasure in living and increases our negative thoughts?"

77

The quester who says that he has practised this and done that without any observable result, who is discouraged and depressed in consequence, has often failed to make any real effort to cleanse his body by reforming its habits.

78

I may know that the world is *maya*, illusion, that the body's desires are for things that pass away within a few minutes or a few years, but food can be very enjoyable and the body's life very comfortable, despite this knowledge!

79

The confusion of religious thinking on this matter is age-old. Yet the issue is quite simple. While we are alive the body is of grave importance but when we are dead it is of no importance at all. Those who condemn, despise, or minimize the body are premature.

80

The kind of asceticism which considers the body as an enemy to the spirit, is a kind of sickness. The two dwell together, belong to one another, and in a proper life co-operate together. To consider them otherwise, to torment the body in order to gain the spirit's favour, is to twist the very meaning of its existence.

81

It is not God who asks would-be saints to do nasty things to their bodies but their own mental imbalance and excess of misplaced fanatic zeal.

82

Buddha of old and Schopenhauer of modern times told men that their misery was inescapable. Neither of them paid one-quarter the attention to his physical body that he paid to his metaphysical reflection. One wonders how much their views might have been modified, if their bodies had been brought by keen and consistent exercise to dynamic vigour and abounding health.

83

The body is our enemy only if we let it tyrannize over the finer aspirations, if we indulge it beyond its real needs and in violation of its real instincts.

84

The student who adopts drastic ascetic disciplines before he is ready for them is likely to have to modify his ascetic ideals or else accept a revised estimate of his strength and limitations.

85

Marie Corelli wrote in the Preface to her novel *The Life Everlasting*: "The Fountain of Youth and the Elixir of Life were dreams of the ancient mystics but they are not dreams today. To the soul that has found them, they are divine realities. If Man were to learn that he can prolong his life on this earth in youth and health for an indefinite period in which days and years are not counted, he could pass from one joy to another." Yet the author of these lines, and of similar passages in the same book, died at a normal age, despite her bold assertions of a secret knowledge and an exceptional power possessed by her and her teachers. And so died other claimants as honourable and respected as Miss Corelli was, such as Sri Aurobindo and many a Tantrik guru in India and Tibet, as well as dishonourable ones. Nobody has historically succeeded in robbing Nature of her power to inflict death. But there is another aspect of this topic which throws some light on it.

86

When the body of Father Charles de Foucald was exhumed, one year after burial, for transfer to another site, his friend General Laperrine was astonished to find that the body was without any break and the face quite recognizable, whereas of the two Arab guards murdered at the same time and buried near him only a little dust remained. One of the native soldiers then said, "Why are you astonished that he is thus preserved, General? It is not astonishing, since he was a great marabout (holy man)."

Foucald was a nineteenth-century Christian hermit of the Saharan desert, who sacrificed social position and fortune for an ascetic existence devoted to prayer, meditation, and service of the poor. His ascetic self-mortification was extremely severe.

To this case there may be added the somewhat similar cases of Swami Yogananda of Los Angeles, and Sri Aurobindo of Pondicherry. The ancient hatha yoga texts promise the successful yogi "the conquest of death." This does not mean he will not die, but that his flesh will not decay after death.

87

We have so intimate a relation to the body in practical life that none of us need be blamed for calling it "me." But metaphysically that indicates an adolescent attitude. We advance towards maturity when we regard it as only a part of "me."

88

This domain of natural living, food reform, and hygiene is infested with cranks, fanatics, extremists, and one-idea devotees, just as the domain of mysticism is. The seeker must be warned against letting himself be deceived by their wild intemperate enthusiasms.

89

So much may depend on so little! The condition of a single organ or of a half-centimeter of gland may curse a man's whole life more than any sorcerer can. The shape of his nose may be so disliked by others that his ambitions are thwarted or his desire for love defeated.

90

Being too short in height is unpleasant, undignified, and unfortunate for a sensitive man. But it is well-countered by invisible compensations.

91

A physiognomist once told me that he considered the mouth more revealing of a man's character than, as commonly believed, the eyes. Is this a fact?

92

How important it is to remember that the fall of temperature in the evenings is an invitation to catch cold. Goethe complained while living in Rome of the care he had to take even in the middle of summer to prevent the realization of this possibility.

93

The joy of owning a physical body comes out most in sexual intercourse, yet the same person will feel disgusted with it under different circumstances and at a different time. The pain of owning a body comes out mostly in ill health, yet the same person may glory in it during a game or a sport.

94

Although some people have found spiritual benefit from sickness because of the enforced retirement to bed or hospital which it demands, or because of the reflections which it brings about the limitations of bodily satisfactions and pleasures, it would be a gross misunderstanding to make this the only way of gaining these insights. Other persons have become so embittered and resentful through sickness that they have suffered spiritual loss. Still other persons who have maintained good health have thereby been able to provide the proper circumstances for spiritual search, study, and meditation.

95

The eye is the reflector of mind, the revealer of a man's heart and the diagnoser of his bodily health.

96

Schopenhauer: "With health, everything is a source of pleasure; without it, nothing else, whatever it may be, is enjoyable." It follows that the greatest of follies is to sacrifice health for any other kind of happiness, whatever it may be—for gain, advancement, learning, or fame, let alone, then, for fleeting sensual pleasure.

97

That the life of deep meditation reduces the need of sleep is shown by the case of the Spanish Saint John of the Cross. Three or four hours of repose at night were quite enough for him.

98

Any new bodily regime can be adopted more quickly and more easily if it is adopted more enthusiastically. Some people play with the thought of it for years but never get actually started on it. Others, frightened into it by some dire necessity or taking to it through strong yearning for its benefits, make up their mind to the point of getting excited about it. For them action is the direct consequence of aspiration.

99

Chemical changes in every cell of his body are the outer physical result of this inner second birth.

100

That word "normal" is a deceptive and even dangerous one to use in these matters. For the human race's present condition is an unevolved and, from the philosophic standpoint, unclean one. To accept this as the norm, the ideal to be attained by individuals, is to prevent growth.

101

Sexual desire, wrathful temperament, and despondent outlook may have their source in the body or in the mind, or in both together. Where the physical origin exists, the physical treatment should be given if a lasting result is to be gained.

102

How proudly and how carefully a cat cleans, washes, and combs its fur coat!

103

A clean body is more responsive to the finer feelings and nobler thoughts. But we must remember that skin cleanness is only a small part of the whole. The intestinal tract, the tissues, and the organs are the larger part.

104

To the extent that he has transgressed the laws of moral, mental, and physical hygiene, to that extent he might reasonably be asked to perform penance in proportion. But Nature is not so exacting as that. She will co-operate with and help him from the moment he repents and *does* some of the required penance.

105

Even if these physical plane methods offer only contributory help and secondary values, they will still be worth using by those who need all the help they can get.

106

Those who want the higher degree of knowledge and peace must buy their way into it. The purchase price is high, no less than abstinence, continence, self-denial, and self-mastery—alike in the realm of thoughts as that of acts.

107

Constipation is specifically blamed as a hindrance to the practice of meditation by some teachers. They require it to be cured before allowing students to proceed with the practice itself. They prescribe certain exercises and dietetic changes to remove the condition.

108

These regimes are intended to remove some obstacles to the occurrence of Glimpses, obstacles which are physical and emotional. They are methods of cleansing body and feelings to permit the intuitive element to enter awareness more easily. They constitute the preliminary part of the Quest, preceding or accompanying meditation. It is better to eliminate bad habits, stop unhygienic ways of living, and cultivate willpower if meditation is to take its full and proper effect.

3

DIET

If he can shed the mummy wrappings of acquired notions, complacent bigotries, and superstitious customs, and look at the problem with fresh eyes, he is more likely to succeed in his quest of truth. If he can re-examine the whole meaning of it as though it were a newly discovered problem, he is more likely to move towards its correct solution. If he will refuse to be intimidated by dietary precedent, and begin to rethink the whole matter of eating's why and wherefore, he will reach astonishing results. For much nonsense about diet has come down to us by ignorant tradition and unthinking inheritance.

2

As one draws closer to the soul of things, he comes more into harmony with Nature. And if he is true to his instinct, he will eat his food more and more as Nature herself produces it.

3

Inferior and even harmful foods have been eaten for so long that most people have become addicted to them and, through habitual use, come to like them. It is true that several of these foods have been part of a civilized diet for generations, but the duration of an error does not make it less an error, and does not justify its continuance. It is a fact worth speculating upon that many groups of early Christians were both mystical and vegetarian. Had they not been ousted by the Emperor Constantine—whose imperialistic political purpose they did not serve—from the official Christianity which he (and not Jesus) established, we might today have seen half the Christian world holding a faith in mystical beliefs and eating fleshless foods. The France of Louis XII saw some remnants of those early sects, such as the Albigenses, Montanists, and Camisards—and no less than one-third of the total population of the country—living as vegetarians. Luigi Cornaro lived to a hundred in Italy on a strictly limited daily quantity of food. Dr. Josiah Oldfield was nearing his hundred when I last visited England and attributed the fact to avoiding eating too much, which he termed "the great evil." He is also an enthusiastic advocate of vegetarianism.

4

We are so much the victims of custom and usage, of habit and convention, that even where we at once perceive this weakness in other persons, we fail entirely to perceive it in ourselves. Emerson, the man who wrote the finest essay on the virtue of nonconformity, who proclaimed, "thus ossification is the fall of man," who became the outstanding American prophet of novel views in religion, was completely conformist and habitarian at home, was still the follower of old views in diet. Whenever he encountered dietetic reform visibly in practice before his eyes, he almost lost his serenity in the vehemence of the scorn which it provoked in him. His was still the compartmentally divided mind; he sought truth in the study room but not in the dining room! He admired reform in one field but despised it in another.

5

The greatest of all diet reforms is the change from meat-eating to a meatless diet. This is also the first step on the spiritual path, the first gesture that rightness, justice, compassion, purity are being set up as necessary to human and humane living, in contrast to animal living.

6

If there is any single cause for which I would go up and down the land on a twentieth-century crusade, it is that of the meatless diet. It may be a forlorn crusade, but all the same, it would be a heart-warming one.

7

We hear often of those who live to a ripe old age in health and in strength, but who eat whatever they fancy and drink what they like; they sin against the laws of health and live without any health regimes or disciplinary controls. This is used as an argument against the latter. But it is a poor argument. For anyone who follows their example takes risks and runs hazards with his health, since theirs is a way based on mere chance and complete uncertainty. They were lucky enough to be blessed by nature with bodies strong enough to resist the ill-treatment thus received or favoured by destiny with recuperative power to ward off its bad effect. If anyone could collect the statistics, they would unquestionably show that for each person who escaped infirmities and lived long in this way, a hundred failed to do so.

8

A meatless diet has practical advantages to offer nearly everyone. But to idealists who are concerned with higher purposes it has even more to offer. On the moral issue alone it tends to lessen callousness to the sufferings of others, men or animals, and to increase what Schweitzer called "reverence for life."

9

A meatless diet is advisable for aspirants, where circumstances permit, as the brain fed on it is less resistant to meditation.

10

The delusion that flesh food is essential to maintain strength dies hard. I do not know a stronger animal than an elephant. I have seen it in the East doing all the work that a powerful steam-crane will do in the West. Yet the elephant is a vegetarian. Moreover it outlives most other animals.

11

Why should we abstain from meat-eating? (a) Cultivated land if planted with vegetables, fruits, and nuts will yield much more food for an over-populated world than it could yield if left under pasture for cattle and sheep. (b) The ghastly work of slaughtering these harmless innocent creatures can be done only by hardened men, whose qualities of compassion and sympathy must inevitably get feebler and and feebler. How many housewives could do their own butchering? (c) In terms of equal food value, the meatless diet costs less. (d) Animals which suffer from contagious diseases pass on the germs of these diseases to those who eat their flesh or parasites. (e) Meat contains excretory substances, purines, which may cause other, non-communicable diseases.

12

Those who would like to be vegetarians for compassionate reasons but feel the need of meat for maintaining strength can find proper substitutes in milk and cheese. These dairy products contain the same animal proteins as meat, and will serve as well to sustain vitality, while being free from the stain of slaughter.

13

Another point for vegetarians is that cruel, wild beasts such as tigers and treacherous, angry reptiles such as snakes live wholly on animal products. The connection between their nature and their food is not entirely coincidental.

14

Nature (God) has given us the grains and seeds, the fruits and plants to sustain our bodies; what we have used beyond this was got by theft. We robbed calves of their milk and bees of their own stored food.

15

Whatever man harms or hurts, he will have to live with for a time until he learns to refrain, until his reverence for life is as active here as anywhere else. This is why the horrors of vivisection will have to be expiated by the man who caused them.

16

Only a heroic and determined few can suddenly reverse the habits of a lifetime and adopt new ones with full benefit. For most people it is more prudent and beneficial to make the change by degrees. Thus, if convinced of the merits of a permanent meatless diet, they can cut down periodically the meats consumed, taking care to replace them by suitable substitutes. If convinced of the curative virtue of a temporary unfired diet, they can eat less cooked and add more vital foods to their meals.

17

Confronted by a totally new set of concepts of living, they irritably shake their heads at its supposed faddism or caustically jeer at its supposed quackery or derisively taunt its advocates with their supposed crankiness.

18

We are called to give others—animals as well as humans—the same treatment that we call on God to give us.

19

When the body has become accustomed through long years of dietary habit to a vegetarian menu, the sudden introduction of flesh foods may lead to nitrogenous poisoning. This is because the body can no longer tolerate a foreign protein. And from this we can understand why lifetime vegetarians, and especially lifelong ones like Indian Brahmins, become sick or suffer from nausea when accidentally or unconsciously, they let a piece of meat slip into their food.

20

The foods that suit him best, he alone can find out. But he should select them from the restricted list with which philosophy will gladly provide him.

21

It is not only that we ought to avoid the dead animals for our food, but also we ought to avoid the products of live animals for this purpose, too. By accepting them for bodily nourishment we accept the influence they contribute to the forming of our nature. Body and mind are intertwined. We can well sustain our lives without milk and its derivatives, just as we can without red flesh, white flesh, fish, and eggs.

22

Scientifically, milk is modified blood and eggs are interrupted chicks.

23

By experiment he may discover what agrees with his stomach and what not. It he notices disagreeable symptoms mentally or physically, such as dull headaches or stomach heaviness, then he should drop this item of food and observe whether there is any difference in his condition. If not, then it is not the food but something else that lies behind the distress.

24

He should not be willing to absorb the psychic characteristics of an animal which come with meat, and more especially with the blood of meat.

25

Our appetites have become perverted, our cravings for food have become morbid. We eat quantities for which the body has no actual need. The conventional dietary habits are false standards by which to live. We could quite well maintain ourselves by eating smaller amounts of rich, concentrated, and stimulating proteins, as well as of clogging starches.

26

Neither meat nor alcohol is indispensable to the body. Neither health nor palate will suffer without them. By slowly reducing their intake—or suddenly, if one prefers and is able to do so—the desire for them will completely vanish in time. But proper substitutes from the dairy or from the plant kingdoms should replace them if this transition is to be comfortable and satisfactory.

27

Nature's restorative power usually tries to heal the body or correct its functions but man's ingrained gluttony, error, ignorance, and self-indulgence usually throw too much obstruction in its way to let this desirable result happen.

28

It is not only the artificial heating of food which deprives it of nutritive, vitalizing, and healing qualities, but even the natural wilting of food does so to a lesser extent. Scientific methods of preserving, refrigerating, or keeping fresh food introduce new evils which destroy the value of their benefits.

29

There is no objection to gratifying the palate; indeed it is quite natural to do so. But when it happens at the expense of spiritual and physical well-being, then it reaches a point when it does become objectionable and unnatural. The cravings of the palate are not what they ought to be but what, hereditarily and artificially, they have been made to be.

30

When it comes to combining the technical knowledge of biology with spiritual insight, the change of viewpoints makes it necessary to modify and even correct the scientific knowledge. That milk provides a better way to get animal protein than meat is perfectly correct; but to accept what is taught by science, that we need animal protein, is wrong. This is not so, but the long continued habits of the human race have made it seem so.

31

The statement of physiology that tissues must be fed with protein to repair their waste is a greatly exaggerated dogma. They need but little—a couple of ounces are enough. What the average man eats is far too rich in protein, so the system must set itself to work getting rid of this surplus, thus increasing waste products and unnecessarily spending vitality.

32

The psychic effects of meat-eating are undesirable. If those who believe that they cannot sustain life without it could see these effects, and if they had to be their own butchers, how many would continue this habit?

33

Protein is protein, whether extracted from animals or plants. It does not alter its chemical composition if its source is transferred from one of these to the other.

34

The protein myth needs deflating. The cow eats no protein at all, only grass and fodder, yet it produces milk which is converted into high protein cheese. I have lived on a diet of fresh fruits and some rye crackers for more than a year at a time and maintained my normal weight throughout the period.

35

If he cares enough for the Quest and understands enough about the relation between it and diet, he will come sooner or later to choose his food with more resistance to habit.

36

There is some confusion here both in the arguments of advocates and the criticisms of objectors. It is not possible for any man completely to avoid taking the life of all other creatures in the animal kingdom, especially tiny creatures like microorganisms. But it is possible for him to avoid taking the lives of larger creatures which possess larger, more delicate nerve systems, and causing suffering to them unnecessarily.

37

Never before have there been so many deaths from diseases of the blood vessels including the largest of them all—the heart. Why? The introduction of larger quantities of meat into the diet has led to the introduction of larger quantities of other animals' blood into the body.

38

If you are to be a guest, it is no great trouble to either you or your host, to warn him in advance about the prohibited foods.

39

Early in human history, milk was disdained as an article of food because it was thought to be unnatural for adults to take what Nature supplied to infants.

40

Pythagoras pointed out that the way a nation treated its animals, so far as they are at its mercy, is an indirect judgement of its character.

41

Although sodium chloride salt is unacceptable as an article of diet in its manufactured commercial form, it may be acceptable as a medicinal article when it appears as one of the ingredients of a natural spa spring water. It would then be taken for a short period only and for the therapeutic purpose of assisting in the removal of a bad bodily condition.

42

Smoking is a falsification of the natural instinct of the body to preserve its own inner cleanliness as well as an insult to its sensibility to irritating odours. If smoking is actually enjoyed as a pleasure, that merely shows how false have become the habits imposed on the body's natural instinct. He who desires to rid himself of the smoking habit must therefore restore the operation of this instinct. Among the various techniques that he will have to adopt, one is that of fasting. Short but regular fasts will help to purify him and give back what he has lost—the true instinct of the body and the senses. When this instinct is restored, the desire for smoking will begin to fall away of itself, and indeed an aversion to it will replace it.

43

The intolerance of some aggressive and fanatical opponents of meat-eating, smoking, and alcohol-drinking is itself a vicious attitude which harms them in a different way as much as those bad habits harm their addicts.(P)

44

There is an opportunity to strengthen his will, overcome a bad habit and show his determination to quicken progress by dropping smoking altogether from the first day.

45

Those who light one cigarette after another do not sin against morality; they sin against health.

46

The thirteenth Dalai Lama considered tobacco to be more pernicious and more polluting than alcohol and banned its use not only by the monks and priests but even by the laymen.

47

Alcoholic drink releases the sociability in man, but if taken further it then releases the animality in him.

48

The more materialistic type of person needs heavier food, the more spiritually minded needs lighter more digestible food if he is not to dull his sensitivity.

49

Alcohol is objectionable as a part of human diet particularly when it is used in high concentrations as in brandy, gin, rum, and cocktails. Then it is poisonous physically and morally. But as a medicine for emergencies it is acceptable.

50

During my Mexican experiments, I discovered that a cooked meal dulls the mind and produces a sleepy feeling, but not so with an uncooked one. Now that I live on a mixed diet, I prefer to have the cooked meal at night so that the sleepiness comes at the right time.

51

It is not only the unnecessary killing of tamed animals for food that shows man's thoughtless lack of mercy, but also the unnecessary hunting and killing of wild animals. They are entitled to their mountain or forest home.

52

Bodhidharma, the founder of Zen, was not the only person who nourished himself with dried tea leaves. A few years after the end of the American Civil War, John Muir—geologist and genius, nature lover and explorer—carried for food only bread and dried tea leaves while climbing the high Sierra Nevada Mountains overlooking the Yosemite valley. He did this quite often and kept a sturdy health, which shows that the legend about Bodhidharma's diet may not have been so mythical after all.

53

It is a task heavy enough to stimulate spiritual intuitions in our era without adding the extra burden involved in correcting false appetites at the table. That is a thankless task which incites the greatest impatience in others and the greatest reluctance in oneself. One instinctively shirks becoming a dietary iconoclast overturning the ancient and beloved idols of whole peoples. For no habits are so hard to uproot as eating habits, none so much a part of ingrained human nature.

54

There is no universal maximum of the amount of food and frequency of meals. That depends on the man's type and on his activity. Each must find out what keeps him most efficient.

55

The harmful effects of tea drinking upon the heart's action, the tissues of the stomach, the digestion of starch and protein cannot be denied. The accumulated effects of its poisoning of the body are serious.

56

Many students raise the question of excessive smoking and cocktail drinking. There was plenty of excuse for the former during the war. It is not serious psychically, although bad for health physically. Cocktail drinking is, however, inadvisable for the student who begins to make progress on the path. All strong spirits like whisky and gin, or liquors like brandy, are definitely harmful to him because he is bound to have become more sensitive than when he began the Quest. What was all right for him in the past is not so now for he has advanced since then. The further purification of the self must proceed to make possible the further illumination of the self. He may find it helpful to overcome these physical habits of smoking and drinking by taking short fasts of about one complete day in duration. During each fast he should drink water mixed with fruit juice. Two or three such days per month would help to strengthen the higher will and to weaken the undesirable habits. And of course he should pray daily for the strength to overcome them. Indeed, prayer for the Overself's Grace in this connection is most important.

57

One good way to serve others is by shopkeeping, and a still better way is to make one's shop a health food store. In the latter case, one is doing more than merely earning a living, since he will be rendering a specially needed service in his community. Health foods are, in many cases, a vast improvement over ordinary foods, and useful to supplement the meatless diet.

58

Animals live in the herd instinct. They do not possess self-consciousness as individualized human beings possess it, nor have they the capacity of aspiring to what is above their own level. But they are subject to evolution and will ultimately arrive at our level. Kindness to those nearest the human stage promotes their evolution into its best side. Cruelty to them launches them into its worst side and punishes us with a karma of criminal primitive classes of the lowest order.

59

The eating of meat is a remnant of primitive demon-worship, when animals were sacrificed on temple altars to these unseen and unholy creatures. The initiated among the early Christian Fathers knew this well. In *The Spiritual Crisis of Man*, I have already stated Saint John Chrysostom's opinion of meat-eating as being "unnatural" and "of demoniacal origin" while Origen wrote, "Do not flatter the demons by means of sacrifices."

60

There is far too much ignorance among educated people—so how much more among the others—of the heavy contribution made to the causes of sickness by faulty eating habits and by dietary deficiencies.

61

The wisdom of the World-Mind has put quick-lines into the animal mind—which you may call instincts if you wish—which show it how to keep alive by picking out the food needed. Man, being the possessor of an animal body, shares a proportion of these instincts; for the rest he must use his judgement.

62

Only good positive thoughts were allowed to enter his head and good meatless food his stomach.

63

It is a fact, which some clairvoyants have observed and which scientific researches by the late Sir J. Bose in Bengal and Cleve Backster using polygraph technique in New York have confirmed, that plants feel and that they have intelligent responses which on a human level would be emotional. This has in fact been advanced as a defense of meat-eating and against those practising meat avoidance. My reply is that the plant form is not so sensitive as the animal form, lacking so highly developed a nerve system. It suffers—but less.

64

It is necessary to eat living things as food in order to keep living ourselves. That is not a matter of our choosing but a necessity forced upon us by Nature or God. We have no freedom in the choice. But we are free to reduce the area of our destructiveness and to lessen the amount of pain we inflict. It is less destructive to uproot a vegetable or pluck a fruit than to slay an animal—and there is less suffering too. This is the answer to the argument that we still destroy life when we become vegetarians.

65

If we could examine the prehistoric period of man, and not merely his latest century, we would find that the duration of his life has since been shortened, while the condition of his body has deteriorated through new diseases. The cause in both cases lies in his changed feeding habits to some extent, and in his unrestricted sexual habits to a much larger extent.

66

Where man has given himself up to sexual excitement as a continuing and enduring feature of his life—as contrasted with the wild animals which experience it only at particular seasons—the cause exists not in the different nature with which he has been endowed but in the excess of strongly nutritive material which has absorbed into his body. To prove that this is so, one has only to take the case of his domestic animals which, when also getting superfluous nutriment, are excited more often than the wild ones.

67

Foods which stimulate sexual activity include eggs, oysters, chocolate, and meat.

68

The extractive substances of red fish like salmon and carp and red meats like beef and venison irritate the vital tissues and raise blood pressure. This in turn raises sexual desire. White meat and white fish are less liable to do this.

69

Diet alone will not be enough to bring sexual function under control, but only helps to do so. Otherwise, the rabbit would not be so unchaste. Climate is not less important, for the flesh-eating Eskimo living in Arctic regions is sexually lethargic whereas the vegetarian native of tropical regions is not.

70

Our definition of sin needs widening. It is also sinful to break the laws of hygiene, to indulge in habits that are either poisonous or devitalizing, to eat foods obtained by slaughter.

71

If the grains, fruits, cereals, and vegetables which we eat are themselves undernourished because the soil in which they grow is deficient in minerals or otherwise exhausted, then we in turn will not really receive from our food the proper nourishment we believe it is giving nor will the cattle pastured on such depleted soil. Nor is this all. If the foods derived from unbalanced soil are our mainstay for a lengthy period of years, the unbalance will be reflected in our body as some kind of sickness or malfunction.

72

Wherever and whenever meatless diet becomes the rule, and not the rarity that it is today, we may expect violence and crime to abate markedly.

73

The changeover from a meat diet to a vegetarian one creates in some cases a feeling of bodily weakness. This will be limited to the transition period only, which may be a matter of days or months, depending on the individual. Such persons should make the changeover gradually. Many others have made the change quite abruptly without any fatigue or any harm.

74

The person who is afraid to alter his living habits, and especially his eating and drinking habits, because he is afraid that other persons may regard him as queer, eccentric, or fanatic forgets that the ownership of his body, the responsibility for its well-being, belongs to him, not them.

75

Some men who have shivered at the thought of inaugurating these reforms or conforming to these regimes came nevertheless to do so in later years. Why? Because they were given a strong enough incentive. Attacked by heart disease, they were warned by physicians to abandon salt; suffering from different sicknesses, they had to abandon meat; others who were gluttons were ordered to curb their meals to more modest proportions. Here the incentive of avoiding earlier death enabled them to accept an abhorred discipline.

76

Emerson, with all his admirable wisdom, was yet not wise enough to attend to his diet. He regularly ate too much cold pie and suffered from indigestion. But what was worse, he ate beef and thus set a bad example to others. His mind was so well purified and so strongly concentrated within the Good, the True, and the Beautiful that it was not affected, whatever happened to his body. But the minds of others were muddier and weaker. A correct example would have been better for them.

77

After some weeks on an uncooked food diet, the intellectual type of person will find, as I found, that there is greater mental clarity and greater mental drive. In fact, there may even be a tendency to overwork intellectually in reading or writing. A century ago, John Linton, of England, reported the result of a long period on such a diet in these words: "I was able to write with an ease and perspicacity and satisfaction which I had never before known, or had any idea of."

78

Nobility of character will not save a man who eats meat from the dark karma which he thereby makes, although it may modify it. This bad habit puts his good health into peril.

79

The movement is a circular one. Bad eating habits can produce an excess of bile. This in turn produces depression, irritability, a critical view of people and events. On the other hand, the man who starts with such a view will finish with an excess of bile, too. This is why philosophic disciplines are directed toward both the body and the mind, not to one alone.

80

A glass of wine which might upset the mental balance of a beginner, and to that extent cause him to forget his quest or create inability to meditate, might leave no more mark on an advanced man than a wave hurling itself upon a rock.

81

The established alimentary errors of the modern way of living—that is, the artificial way—may be partially corrected by eating more fresh fruits and vegetables. It is unfortunate, however, that the commercial definition of freshness does not coincide with Nature's. Therefore we must be more fastidious and selective when buying these foods. This correction is needed by all victims of civilization; it does not matter whether they come to it because of food chemistry's revelation of the need of dietary vitamins or because of mystical philosophy's revelation of the need of return to nature.

82

The *Bhagavad Gita*, India's manual for yogis since the most ancient times, prescribes that the food for spiritual practitioners should be light and digestible. Why? Because the body's condition does throw its influence into the mind's condition. A body which is habitually constipated, whose bowels are tight and filthy with accumulations, receives and spreads morbid poisons. These affect, in time, not only the organs directly concerned but also the sexual organs, the blood, brain, and nerves. Lust is stimulated, negative ideas are intensified.

83

The follower of a fleshless diet who throws his principles to the four winds in a trying situation lest he be thought peculiar, eccentric, different, is more eager to please other men than the Overself, more interested in what their opinion is of him than in the success of his quest. How easy it is to make concessions, to give in to the herd expectations! How hard to go all the way with one's convictions, to keep one's link with integrity unbroken. Yet faithfulness is the only attitude for the man who has felt this practical pity for dumb animals.

84

If he really believes in this teaching, he will seek to bring it into every area of his life. There is no area from which it can rightly be left out, not even from that of the kind of food he eats.

85

What really happens is that the body remembers having been fed at certain hours and with certain foods. These memories have been integrated into its subconsciousness and provide the real source of the urge to repeat the experience. The habit is really mental but appears physical.

86

Where rennet is used in the making of cheese, the final product is no longer purely vegetarian. Where eggs are part of a diet, the animal life they contain, even though it is only incipient, violates the vegetarian principle of living.

87

Those who feel it necessary to include eggs in their otherwise vegetarian diet, should confine themselves to sterile eggs which can never be hatched.

88

The sin of gluttony does not necessarily mean eating too much food. It may also mean eating too rich food even when the quantity is not excessive.

89

Mustard, pepper, and paprika stimulate sex organs.

90

It is proper to defend one's life when it is menaced by aggressive men or by wild beasts, but it is against philosophic ethics to take life without a just cause, as when one kills animals for food—still more when one kills them wantonly for sport. Every higher instinct urges us to substitute compassion for cruelty in our dealings with the lower kingdom.

91

The aspirant who fails to practise non-injury sets up an evil relationship which will have to be worked out later, a relationship which will block his entry into the state of lasting enlightenment until it is so worked out. The unnecessary taking of animal life for his food is one form, although a common one, of violation of this ethic.

92

Although he need not go out of his way to appear different from anyone else, although he must effect that compromise with society which will enable him to live in it as necessity dictates he must, he need not become so subservient to the social codes or subscribe so timidly to the social practices that he is willing to slaughter innocent animals for food just because everyone else is doing it. In this matter there can be no surrender, no frightened conformity with barbarous habits. In this respect he will see that the civilization in which he finds himself has not fully outgrown the savage elements. Its progress in social manners and technical efficiency is one-sided.

93

Diet depends on the type of person as well as the stage of development. The contemplative introvert intuitive type needs a fruitarian diet. The physical extrovert type needs a complete heavy protein diet. The best guide to the diet suited to each individual is the *Gita* rule, plus his own instinct, modified by such factors as climatic conditions around him, local availability of foods, and so on.

94

There is a tradition that live snails crawled all over and wholly covered the Buddha's head to prevent his getting sunstroke when he had fallen into deep inner absorption in a place where no tree branches gave their usual shelter. Whether this is true or not, it does convey the idea that the apostle of mercy and love for the whole animal kingdom received his own love reflected back to him by members of that kingdom.

95

The yogi who lives in contented isolation from the burdens and worries of family existence is not helpful to the poor fellow who has to till the field and produce the grain with which to feed him. For, from some source or other, he has to be fed whether he lives in cave or jungle. He cannot live on roots and barks and leaves; that is a pretty fiction for fables and fairy tales. He needs rice or wheat or milk and vegetables, and probably some fruits.

96

The beautiful coloured fruits which the trees and bushes offer him have been saturated with beneficent solar rays, not with innocent blood.

97

What is the answer to the question, Can we offer a meatless diet to pet animals? We can, provided hardboiled eggs and milk are included in the diet. The pet dog or cat will grow just as healthy and have all the strength it needs. But it is very difficult to succeed in limiting it to such a diet unless it is started from the time when it is a little puppy or kitten.

98

Exaggerated notions of the value of the vegetarian diet must be discounted. It will not *of itself* suffice to keep a man healthy or free from the lower passions.

99

If it be asked why abstention from meat-eating should be conducive to sexual self-control, the answer must include a few assertions to be complete. But the prime reason is because most of the animals which are killed and eaten by man owe their own existence to the sexual lust of their parents and this lust permeates their flesh in an invisible psychic-magnetic aura. Most fish of course are an exception to ordinary sexual birth, yet shellfish are a notoriously aphrodisiac article of food. The cause of this must be sought elsewhere than in their origin.

100

Salt is unnecessary in the diet. Most people have a large salt intake from sheer habit, which in turn makes it seem almost a necessity for their bodies. Spiritual aspirants are much better off without salt; it is an artificial irritant that erects additional barriers to progress. Science believes that salt intake is necessary in hot weather to replenish what is lost through the body's perspiration. The fact remains that the salt would not be lost if it were not consumed in the first place; this is the real cause of this vicious circle.

101

The custom which prevailed so widely on vanished Atlantis of offering animals and slaughtering prisoners during the periodical religious rituals, and which was carried over by the survivors into African, American, and Asiatic civilizations of historic times, has died out as purer and more rational concepts of religion have risen. But the custom of offering animals to please not a divine being but a human one, is just as prevalent today as the stupid Atlantean barbarity formerly was. Men still breed hapless four-legged creatures by the million only to slay them in the end and serve them at meals. Such destruction is carried out without feeling, without conscience, and without real necessity. And what right does any of these human beings have to destroy the existence of such a multitude of creatures who have their own place, function, and purpose in the divine World-Idea? In claiming for himself such a right, man arrogantly proclaims himself wiser than his Creator and in disturbing the creation itself by his bloody habits of eating, he violates sacred laws for which he is duly punished. His health suffers, his passions are never allayed, and his violence in war is never ended.

102

Those who believe that a meatless diet must be a flabby and tasteless one believe wrongly. It is quite possible for a vegetarian or a vegan or even a fruitarian to enjoy meals, to find them appetizing and satisfying.

103

If every slaughterhouse were razed to the ground and orchards, thickly planted with fruit-bearing trees, replaced them, all would benefit in the end—including those unfortunate men who earn their livelihood from such slaughter.

104

Food does not directly supply energy but its presence in the body during the process of metabolism acts as a channel for energy to be set free in the body. This is why those who fully undergo the purificatory processes of the Quest and thus regenerate their body, not only need less food than others do, but subsist on finer forms of food.

105

If too much protein is undesirable because it ends in toxic products and destructive acids, too little is also undesirable because it ends in insufficient weight and lessened strength.

106

He alone is entitled to ask for help or mercy—which is a form of help—who himself shows pity, spares life, eschews cruelty, and grants mercy to the helpless and oppressed, who does not, in Plutarch's phrase, "allow his lips to touch the flesh of a murdered being."

107
Mushrooms belong to that order in Nature to which parasites, fungus, and bacteria belong.

108
Grace before meals is like a blessing upon murder, when the meal is part of an animal which has been hunted down by a group of sportsmen helped by bloodthirsty hounds.

109
So long as their plant, grain, vegetable, and fruit food is mass-produced and grown with artificial chemical or animal manure fertilizers and later sprayed with poisons, so long will true health be impossible for city dwellers. For requisite vitamins and minerals will either be lost—destroyed by these wrong methods which serve commercial interests only—or else ill-balanced because too rich in some nourishing elements and too poor in others.

110
Because the flesh of dead animals and the eggs of living bodies have no true affinity with the bodies of human beings, who exist on a higher level, they are unfit for use as foods by those beings.

111
Foods which cause clogging of the intestines are either of a starchy character (white flour is used to make wallpaper hanger's paste) or composed of gristle and bones (carpenter's glue is made from them) or of fatty oily character (observe how they cling to the inside of a frying pan when cold). To reduce the use of such foods is very desirable.

112
The raw food cure is a form of mono-diet which offers most of the advantages of moderate fasting without its disadvantages. By careful choice during the first part of the cure there can be used only foods with eliminative properties, serving equivalently to a fast; while during the second part a different kind, having upbuilding properties, can be used.

113
It is an ancient knowledge although a neglected modern one, that many vegetables and fruits have strong medicinal properties.

114
He does not eat meat, not so much because he thinks it poisons the body, but more because he feels pity for slaughtered animals. He does not drink alcohol because he believes it would interfere with the efficiency of his work, and much more because of his spiritual effort at self-conquest. He does not smoke, first because he regards smoking as physically un-healthy, and second because his body becomes so refined as to feel a

physiological reaction of strong nausea to it. Thus, these three renunciations are both preoccupations with bodily welfare and with ethical ideals; indeed, they are actually tokens of his balanced ideals.

115

What applies to the place of the body applies consequently to the foods eaten to maintain the body. Because they leave some effect upon the mind through the nerve system and the brain, foods are classified into three kinds by the yogis. Anyone can see the reason for this in the case of some foods and drinks like alcoholic liquors, which stimulate the passions. There are other foods which have a calming influence on the mind.

116

It is unfortunately largely true, this accusation that vegetarians are often drab creatures, that vegetarian restaurants are not seldom dreary places, and that vegetarian meals are often tasteless and unsustaining. But this need not be.

117

We may fast for a few days but we must eat for a whole lifetime.

118

Nature (God) has given men the plants whence to draw the food needed to keep them alive. But few seem to notice that these were given to them raw, not cooked. Men egotistically try to better the gift, to their own detriment and disease.

119

In the early stages of an unfired diet, unpleasant symptoms of elimination such as headaches may appear—just as in fasting. They are to be welcomed, not regretted.

120

To convert barley into beer and grapes into brandy is to destroy the gifts of Nature. Yet this is done every year to the extent of millions of tons. There is a penalty in human degradation and human misery for this.

121

Meat is a very putrefactive food: it decays quicker than vegetables or grains. If it is not digested and passed out of the body in a normal period, this putrefactive quality may lead to certain diseases. This is why vegetarians suffer less from these diseases than meat eaters.

122

The disciplined abstinence from prohibited or undesirable foods is not to be made into a source of self-torment.

123

Saint Paul on vegetarianism: "I will eat no flesh for evermore, that I make not my brother to stumble." (1 Cor. 8:13)

124

The difficulties of keeping to his own rigid mode of protective habit usually become too much in the end for a fastidious traveller. Sooner or later, he succumbs to them and has to give way to the polluting drinking vessels, contaminating eating plates, and meat-smelling restaurants of the non-Brahmin castes. An iron will and inflexible determination to hold to one's regime is needed.

125

It is a mistake to take a meal when mentally tired or emotionally disturbed. The benefit of food intake will be offset by the harm of upset digestion.

126

His experiments in dietary reform must come to this end: he will find that he returns to the philosophic admonition of expertly balanced feeding, but with some better understanding of what constitutes "balance." Formerly, the ingredients of his raw salads were limited to lettuce, cucumber, and cress. He will add other raw vegetables such as peas, red cabbage, squash, and even vegetable roots such as carrot, celeriac, parsnip, and beets—grated, of course, or he could not endure them, and rendered palatable with tasty dressings. Formerly he mixed indiscriminately fruit, raw and cooked vegetables together at the same meal. Now he will try to keep them apart and eat them at separate meals.

127

How free from hard toil in the fields would the wide adoption of a fruitarian diet render the life of man! How independent of farm equipment and tools, kitchen stoves, fuel, appliances, utensils, and all the other paraphernalia with which he burdens himself!

128

They will one day feel mercy for the animals and desist from the custom of slaughtering, cooking, and eating them. Of course, the slaughter is done indirectly, by others acting on their behalf. But some of the guilt remains.

129

Even water taken to excess may lead to death, even beneficial vitamins also. Thus science knows from tests with animals that almost any food item or product can be fatal if too much too quickly is eaten or drunk. This verifies my often used phrase that "a good overdone becomes the bad."

130

The vegetarian who refuses to turn his body into a graveyard for slaughtered animals is obeying not only a moral law but also a hygienic and an aesthetic one.

131

Appetite has really become an artificial and abnormal thing, having taken the place of true hunger, which alone is natural. The one is a sign of bondage but the other, of freedom.

132

It may be considered folly by common opinion but this refusal to destroy life unnecessarily, this reverence for it, must become a deeply implanted part of his ethical standard.

133

If the body is intolerant of particular treatments and allergic to particular foods, it should not be forced to accept them.

134

The time has come to arouse the conscience of all those who sincerely seek the Good and the Right to their duty in the matter of slaughtering innocent animals, a conscience which, if it could speak unperverted by racial habits, would emphatically repeat the Mosaic commandment, "Thou shalt not kill."

135

There are cruelties practised on animals to gain food for man, dress for women, entertainment and medicinal drugs for both. The human claim of necessity as a justification is a mistaken one.

136

There are two groups who go even farther than the vegetarians. One eats only the fruit of trees and so are called fruitarians. The other abstains from dairy produce but still eats vegetables and so are called vegans.

137

To put the body under a necessary discipline is not the same as putting it under an unnecessary tormenting asceticism. Those who cry out that the body is being maltreated when it is no longer fed with red meat, or gorged with excessive food, or poisoned with fiery liquor, cry a false alarm.

138

It is true that Gandhi drank milk but the fact always troubled his conscience.

139

The legumes are much favoured by vegetarians because they are rich in protein and palatable in taste. But they are also gas-producing and somewhat indigestible. If eaten at all, they should be taken in small quantities.

140

I have scooped up the inside of many an avocado—an excellent food— and spread much tahini on many slices of bread.

141

A Japanese guru told his disciple that he would have to wait twelve months for enough purification to prepare the way for his sanctification.

During that time, his efforts should proceed strenuously, and they were not only to be concerned with the thoughts themselves but also with the physical intake, solid and liquid.

142

In this matter it is better to be fastidious, and to reject much that is offered.

143

As his mind becomes purer and his emotions come under control, his thoughts become clearer and his instincts truer. As he learns to live more and more in harmony with his higher Self, his body's natural intuition becomes active of itself. The result is that false desires and unnatural instincts which have been imposed upon it by others or by himself will become weaker and weaker and fall away entirely in time. This may happen without any attempt to undergo an elaborate system of self-discipline on his part: yet it will affect his way of living, his diet, his habits. False cravings like the craving for smoking tobacco will vanish of their own accord; false appetites like the appetite for alcoholic liquor or flesh food will likewise vanish; but the more deep-seated the desire, the longer it will take to uproot it—except in the case of some who will hear and answer a heroic call for an abrupt change.

144

The animal in a slaughterhouse or being hunted by a pack of hounds accompanying a sportsman is full of fear. This affects the adrenaline glands which pass toxic material into the body. Whoever eats the meat of that animal may be getting protein and strength, but he also gets undesirable material.

145

Have they no pity on the lambs torn away from their mothers' sides (as I have seen in New Zealand) to be slain and exported to satisfy the appetite of humans?

146

The killing instinct in men shows itself first in their diet and after this in their perpetual wars. Even when Rome became Christian the gladiatorial shows were continued as the cockfights were in Protestant England and bullfights in Catholic Spain.

147

It is philosophically advantageous to preserve a comprehensive equanimity amid the vicissitudes of human fortune and to practise a reasonable indifference toward *outer conditions*. But it is inhuman and unreasonable to demand, as the price of spiritual peace, that we shall renounce all earthly satisfactions to the point of neither enjoying delicious food nor feeling aversion to repulsive food—a rule set down in the chief manual of yoga.

148

Those who sin against their body in order to keep the good opinion of others, or to appear sociable or convivial, commit the further sin of being weak, insincere, and fearful.

149

Several nuts, but not all, are excellent sources of protein to replace that which is lost through abandoning meat. Their indigestibility will disappear if they are finely ground in a mill or made raw into a butter.

150

How necessary it is to test theory by result in these matters of diet is exemplified in many cases like that of Metchnikoff, who propounded the yogurt-way of achieving abnormal longevity and followed it himself, only to die within three years from the diseased bowel condition which his unbalanced fanaticism produced.

151

Eating food of a special kind or sitting in an isolated cave cannot of itself make anyone spiritually minded. But it can lessen the number of obstacles in the way of anyone who seeks to become spiritually minded.

152

The sensitive and humane person who does not pause to consider his guilt in this matter has let himself take the easy conscience-drowning way, partly because it is the popular way and partly because he is duped by a science and religion which are blindly playing the ego's game.

153

Fresh fruits should be tree-ripened. Dried fruits should be naturally or sun-dried, but if a process must be used it should be the low-heat one. Grains, nuts, fruits, and vegetables provide a complete diet for man.

154

The work of bringing the multitudes into adopting a non-flesh diet, and into abandoning harmful habits, ought to be freed from unwise presentation. It ought to be persuasive education, and not vehement propaganda. The case for it ought to be presented temperately and prudently, not aggressively and fanatically.

155

He must find out by personal experience what his stomach can easily digest, and strictly take nothing else. This is one rule. He must eat of such foods no more than his body really needs, which is always less than what custom and society have suggested he needs.

156

Whatever we eat beyond that which the body really needs, gives no strength and yields no benefit. Instead, it actually harms us. Instead of strengthening, it weakens us. Instead of benefiting, it poisons us.

157

How can the human race avoid the fate of being slaughtered in war when it itself slaughters so many innocent creatures in peace?

158

The exploitation of other living creatures to gain unnecessary human food, must be protested against. Forcing their enslavement to human service and slowly distorting their bodies into having unnatural exaggerated functions is a crime against them.

159

Those animals which have lived in the society of man can sense his intent enough to fear death when he takes them to the slaughterhouse.

160

Is the peaceable man to reduce or stop violent aggression against his fellow men but to continue it against other fellow creatures? What about the animals? We are not entitled to destroy animal life without an adequately necessary and morally justifiable purpose. Therefore it is well to enquire from the wise and good into the character of such purposes, and be guided by their counsel rather than by environmental custom. For the latter has led us, through its utter ignorance and total unawareness of the higher laws, into a situation where blow after blow falls heavily upon the human race. Why should we be so astonished that peace is so hard to obtain, that all too often flaming violence of war and death and mutilation is carried across the land despite our prayers to God and our plans to the contrary? So long as millions of innocent animals are bred only to be sent to the slaughterhouses for our unnecessary food, so long will Life pay us in like coin. The lower characteristics are taken into the body, the blood, the nerves, and the brain. They become a part of us. The mind's response to higher ideals is dulled. The passions which make for strife and thence for war meet with less opposition from conscience and reason. The fear, suspicion, fright, and desire for self-protection which contribute toward war, being impregnated into the blood of our meat during the moments preceding its slaughter, are little by little brought into us too through the glands, the nervous system, and the brain, as our own blood feeds them in turn. It would be desirable, although admittedly difficult, gradually to adopt a meatless diet as a help to secure both the individual's development and the world's peace.

Comments on customs

161

Everything is polarized, whether in the visible universe, or in the invisible forces of life itself. This is what the Hindus call the pairs of opposites and the Chinese call the Yin and Yang. All things are complementary and compensatory, yet at the same time antagonistic. If Yang gives us energy, Yin gives us calm. Both are necessary. The macrobiotic cult has also brought this principle into the diet, but they have done it in a fanatical way, with the consequence that they make the largest part of the daily diet a cereal, which leads to excess of starch and of acidity. Also, they use too much sea salt, which leads to a corrosive effect internally. Finally, like the Indians, they do most of their cooking with oil, which places too much strain upon the liver. We should seek balance in diet as in study.

162

Saint Anthony, founder of Christian monasticism and father of Christian anchoreticism, laid down a rule for himself to eat only once a day, and that after the sun had set. But the Buddhist rule for monks is to eat the last meal at midday when the sun is at its highest point! Can we not see here as in so many other spiritual matters, how much human opinion governs men—and not divine inspiration!

163

Peasants in Germany and Russia, in Bulgaria and China, know the worth of black bread. But with the pseudo-progress and the surrender to appearances rather than to honest values, its replacement by whiter and whiter bread is possible, perhaps probable.

164

Many spiritual aspirants who are practising yoga in India usually prepare their own food. The theory is that the magnetic influence of the person who prepares the food affects the latter, and the aspirant eating food permeated with bad magnetism suffers thereby.

The advanced yogis do not need to be too concerned about this, as they are more immune in some ways, although more sensitive in others. But where they have the choice they will be careful in this matter.

165

A saying of the Buddha: "It is not the eating of meat which renders one impure, but being brutal, hard, pitiless, miserly." This passage was directed against those Brahmins who boasted of their faithfulness to external rites.

166

Just as Buddha protested to the Hindu priests against the sacrifice of innocent goats on religious altars, so Jesus protested to the Israelite rabbis against the sacrifice of innocent lambs on religious altars. But where Buddha, in his opposition to all ritual, suggested no substitute, Jesus suggested the eating of bread in place of the lamb's flesh and the drinking of a little red wine in place of the lamb's blood.

167

Jesus' criticism of dietary concern was directed to those orthodox Hebrews who ostentatiously took every care to free their meat from blood as prescribed by their religion, but took little care to free their hearts and minds from selfish, materialistic, or unworthy thoughts and feelings.

168

It has been asked why the Pythagorean teaching interdicted the use of beans in a vegetable diet. Having sojourned and studied in India, Pythagoras was well acquainted with the *Bhagavad Gita*'s rule that the yogi's food should be light and easily digestible. He gave exactly the same rule to his followers. Dried beans fell under the ban because they were then, as now—because of their tough skins—notoriously indigestible. A further reason was his belief, also picked up in India, that all large and medium size beans contain an ingredient which is harmful to the body. The very small bean called "gram" in India and "Mung bean" in China does not fall under the ban: it is harmless, nourishing, and palatable.

169

Perhaps it was dated thirty-five years ago that I went on a journey with V. Subrahmanya Iyer. We travelled for about ten days through jungles and mountain villages in the depths of Mysore state. On our trip, a yogi who was unknown to us joined the party and stayed with us for a day or two. Later in the first day, the yogi darted to the ground where some creepers were growing in a shady, damp place. He pulled up part of a plant and showed it to me and praised its medicinal merits. Iyer told me it was used by old people to become more youthful and to lengthen life; the yogi told me he used it to treat patients suffering from leprosy, to strengthen the heart and thus prevent attacks, and to purify the blood. He added that it was even useful in the kitchen where, mixed with curry and grated coconut, it improved the taste of food. I could not at the time identify the plant with anything I had seen in the West. In Sanskrit it is Soma Valli, in Tamil it is Vallarai, in Hindi it is Brahmi. Preparations from it are made by the ayurvedic native herbalists and medical practitioners.

170

In the warm climate of southern Italy it is possible to find that vegetables are softer, tenderer, and tastier than in our cold northern climate where they are often stiff and fibrous and even indigestible if eaten raw. Even the Italian peasants themselves in the south will eat them raw when out working in the field. This advantage, of course, is offset by the risks of disease associated with raw foods in the Mediterranean countries—especially the risk of dysentery. But to live anywhere in the Mediterranean is to be able to live much more on raw and therefore more vitaminous food than it is in the colder countries.

171

Strange impossible ideas enter my mind at times. Reason soon bids them take their exit, but now and then a few reappear to haunt me. One of them is this: The Japanese associate with their traditional tea-cult an entry into the atmosphere of spiritual tranquillity. May it not be that the modern British—from whom, and for this particular purpose, I must leave out the Celts of Wales and Cornwall, Scotland, and Ireland—being deficient in metaphysical faculty and mystical temperament, drink their tea in an unconscious and futile attempt to touch the divine stillness by a grossly physical act? For the figures show that they drink more tea per head than any other people in the world, outside Southeast Asia.

172

The eating of onions and garlic is forbidden to the Yellow Hat monks of Tibet—the celibate, stricter order. A monk who has partaken of them is regarded as unclean, and cannot take part in any religious ceremony. He is not even allowed to put out a fire.

173

Many of the monks and porters in Tibet make their lunch of tsampa—which is barley flour mixed with cold water, kneaded into raw dough-like paste, rolled into a ball, and eaten uncooked. The monks have only buttered tea, the porters beer, to complete their lunch. The porters can carry heavy loads on this diet, which is repeated at breakfast and at night. The point to be noted here is that although their work is exceptionally burdensome because of the steep and rocky nature of the mountainous ground over which they often have to travel, they carry it out quite successfully on such raw, uncooked food.

174

Even the two great religious lawgivers who laid down social rules for their followers which allowed a flesh diet, did not allow it absolutely. Muhammed and Moses prohibited pork from being included, while Moses went further and ordered a preliminary process that robs the meat of much of its harm. It is not so much the meat that is harmful and debasing, as its life-force carrier, the blood. Before a Jew eats meat, the blood is almost entirely withdrawn from it, being drained out by a soaking for some hours in salt water.

175

The monks belonging to the thousand-year-old Carthusian Order never eat meat. They model themselves largely on the early Christian monks of Egypt. The Trappist monks of today are also vegetarians.

176

Comte de Saint Germain ate oats for his breakfast. He drank a special herbal tea. He formed the habit in India while gathering knowledge from a certain teaching.

177

The ancient Sanskrit texts give strict rules about eating. They forbid the preparation of food by a member of a caste lower than that of the man who eats it. Even today a Brahmin would rather carry his own food than go into a non-Brahmin restaurant when travelling. On these lines a Westerner should do the same if he cannot find vegetarian food.

178

England pays out an enormous amount of money for the doubtful privilege of buying dead bodies from abroad to feed living men. She could save all that money and thus help to strengthen her situation. And, if she used her arable land entirely for fruit, vegetables, and grain crops instead of cattle grazing or breeding, she would get five or six times as much food from the same ground.

179

During my Asiatic travels a group of Chinese Buddhists asked me to talk to them—an activity which in those days I was willing to do, unlike today. After the spoken address they invited me to dine with them. There were about twenty of us and when tea was served one laughingly remarked that, in contrast to the English, they put no milk in it. I enquired why milk was rejected. He answered that it was distasteful to many, if not most, Chinese because those who drank it were supposed to emit a cowlike odour, while it was repulsive to the Buddhists among them because its human use was a robbery of the calf.

Milk is an animal product but few Western vegetarians seem able to leave it out of their diet and yet remain satisfied. I am one of the few. Their difficulty lies principally in replacing the nutritive substances and calcium minerals which milk and cheese supply and which are necessary to the human body. I believe this difficulty could be met, as the Chinese meet it, by using soyabean milk and soyabean cheese, whose chemical composition is about the same as the animal product. Or a different and suitable replacement could be nut milk, which is easily made either from almond or coconuts. I do not even use this, preferring tahini, the thick fluid derived from sesame seeds.

180

It is a Japanese idea to serve each vegetable separately—and to eat it separately and not to mix all the vegetables together as in the Chinese chop suey (which is after all not a real Chinese dish, but an American invention). This brings out the best taste and flavour of each of the vegetables.

181

Indian widows are made by custom to live a very ascetic existence. Their food is sparse and basic: no spices are allowed in it because it is believed they strengthen sexual instincts.

182

A philosophical view of the matter must discount the value of certain injunctions given by eminent spiritual authorities, such as several traditional Hindu manuals which say "the yogi is to eat what is put before him" (as a sign of his freedom from aversion and attraction), or such as the Japanese Zen master Keizan's rule: "Food exists only to support life: do not cling to the taste of it."

183

Even among the Indian teachers there is lack of agreement on this subject. Although this contradiction may not be known to enthusiastic recent converts, it is bewildering to some of their veteran followers. Swami Brahmananda, a direct disciple of Sri Ramakrishna and first president of the Ramakrishna Order of Monks, declared that it was nonsense not to eat meat. The late Swami Shivananda, second president of the same order and another direct disciple, often smoked tobacco. I remember an anecdote which was told me by His Highness the late Maharaja of Mysore. Swami Vivekananda came to Mysore in quest of financial help for his proposed journey to Chicago to address the 1893 World Parliament of Religions which was destined to bring him sudden fame. My friend's father, the previous Maharaja, immediately recognized the inner worth of the Swami and gladly granted help. He sent one of his palace officials with Vivekananda to the local bazaar with instructions to buy whatever things he wished to have. But despite the official's repeated cajoling, the Swami would not accept anything else than a large cigar which he lit at the shop and seemed to enjoy hugely. Vivekananda ate meat. He even advocated animal food to his fellow Hindus because it would give them more strength and more power as a nation in the fight for its own rights and place. But had the science of nutrition been as advanced in his day as it is now, it could have informed him that all the body building and energizing attributes of flesh food could be obtained from vegetable proteins and carbohydrates.

Sri Yashoda Mai, the female guru, and Sri Krishna Prem of Almora, her male disciple, both smoked. Her Holiness told a North Indian prince that it was not bad to smoke and offered him a cigarette herself. So naturally he smoked it, having received it from such holy hands. "I could not refuse it," the prince told me. This began a course which ended in chain-smoking. I knew him for many years and finally persuaded him to free himself from both smoking and gluttony.

Ramana Maharshi of South India, like most Brahmins of that region, considered meat as too low a form of food to be used by the spiritually minded.

In the West we know that Blavatsky, the Theosophical seer, too often kept her fingers busy rolling long Russian çigarettes. Gurdjieff, the Armenian occultist and one-time teacher of Ouspensky, usually produced packets of cigarettes for his disciples to smoke, whilst himself indulging in oversized cigarettes.

Ralph Waldo Emerson, following the common habit of his time and place, ate animal food. He even poked gentle fun at vegetarians.

4

FASTING

Under the heading of temporary asceticism, the philosophic discipline includes fasting. If done at the right time and for the proper time, it is a mild but useful help to weaken animal desires, curb sex and soften anger, subdue an excessively critical intellect, remove resentment, and bestow serenity. In this way it is also of worth in clearing the mind when in doubt about a correct decision. But to expect the spiritual benefits of a fast to show themselves during the fasting period itself, would be a mistake. The weakness of the flesh may chill all spiritual activity. If it does, then the benefits will start to show as soon as sufficient food has been taken to strengthen the body again.

2

Just as Jesus prepared himself for his coming mission by, among other things, fasting, so did Zoroaster. Muhammed recommended fasting as an atonement and expiation for sin. "Fasting is a shield," he said. In the Jewish religion, Yom Kippur is an annual holy day when every member of that faith has to fast fully for twenty-four hours, not even drinking water, the purpose being to seek forgiveness of past sins. Hence its name, "The Day of Atonement."

3

Although the method of fasting is neither pleasant to contemplate nor agreeable to undergo, the prospect that most of one's bodily troubles and emotional difficulties will respond to it in some degree may help one accept it.

4

To go through the ordeal of fasting the body is not on the same level as flagellating it but on a much higher one. It is sane where the other practice is silly.

5

Fasting is both a penance and a purification, both a source of strength and a method of discipline.

6

The more anyone has practised overindulgence of his senses, the more he needs to undertake the discipline of fasting. In renouncing food and drink, he renounces all the sense-activities which follow after their use.

7

There are times when there is nothing that can be said or written by another that would be useful in helping to lead him out of his apparent spiritual stagnation. It may be something in his way of living or what he eats or drinks which is contributing to the stagnation. If so, there is nothing equal to a few short twenty-four or thirty-six hour fasts to discover what it is, for then the true instincts of the body begin to be restored.

8

The practice of rigid self-denial helps to bring his lower nature under control. The fast is the severest reasonable form which this practice can take.

9

A man arrives more quickly at his own natural instincts and true desires after fasting. With every fast he sheds some part of the artificial and false ones which habit, heredity, society, suggestion, and ignorance have imposed upon him.

10

My twenty-day fast had three interesting consequences apart from the body cleansing which prolonged fasts produce: first, a clearness of thought which was almost intuitive in its correctness; second, an immediacy of understanding which penetrated swiftly the deepest significance of a situation or experience; third, a heightened fluency in the use of words as instruments of expression.

11

If it cleanses the body of accumulated poisons, fasting also cleanses the mind of accumulated errors. This it does by opening a way into the mind for new ideas and preparing it to receive truer ones less resistantly. Thus the fast moves a man away from where he is standing in his own light. It is a negative method of achieving positive results.

12

I have no desire to intrude my writing upon so specialized a field as the cure of disease and healing of sickness. But it is worth incidental noting that there have been many cases where, after undergoing the purificatory regime solely for spiritual reasons, people have been pleasantly surprised to find that it also freed them from bodily ailments.

13

Hippocrates, one of the founders of Greek medical science and practice, which gave so much to modern allopathy, put fasting among the primary remedies. Yet how neglected has it been until lately, until the awakening of old truths reborn under néw names in spiritual, psychic, and physical matters.

14

Fasting gives the body a chance to regain its lost chemical balance.

15

When the supply of food to the body is stopped, and the experiment of fasting is begun, several of the physiological functions will have a chance to rest. The energies which would have been expended on their operations are then set free to cleanse the organs concerned.

16

A fast should improve eyesight because millions of tiny capillaries in the eyes are choked by toxic debris.

17

Through repetitions of the fast, he is able gradually to correct the misleading appetites of the body and straighten the twisted inclinations of the mind.

18

After the fast his taste buds will naturally abandon their perverted condition and adjust themselves to their proper work.

19

Sometimes the diet and the regime take almost instantaneous effect, but more often some time must elapse for the results to show themselves.

20

This need of cleansing the body to make it better serve the mind and obey the spirit, is usually associated with austere asceticism. Yet it was recognized by that lifelong opponent of asceticism, Muhammed. He instituted the regime of fasting from food and drink during the daytime hours of the sacred month of Ramadan. He enjoined a prefatory routine washing of face and feet and arms, mouth and nose and ears, before taking up a position on the prayer mat to commune with God. He prohibited the eating of certain meats and the drinking of alcoholic liquors.

21

The benefits of fasting are not only physical and moral but also psychological, since it enjoins patience and perseverance.

22

During the first phases of an unfired food regime, and still more during the fasting regime, there is often manifested a disinclination towards mystical exercises or meditation, or even an inability to continue their practice. The seeker may take this calmly and without anxiety. It is only a temporary phase, for both inclination and ability are to return at a later date. This is the way in which the subconscious forces prompted by the Overself concentrate their work of purification and renovation upon the body and feelings alone for a time, to gain the most effective results in the shortest time. Thus, those forces which would otherwise be used up in creating the desire to meditate—the atrophy of willpower and the deprivation of energy in this direction need not be fought but should be accepted as a passing and necessary phenomenon.

23

In every system throughout antiquity there was an ascetic preliminary side which purified the mind and body and then only did meditation start. Without such purification, that is, asceticism, all the dangers of meditation—hallucination, misuse of occult powers, egotistic fancies, mediumship, and so on—are free to arise, but with it there is better protection against several of them. This explains why whenever fasting or on unfired food asceticism, there is disinclination for and inability to practise meditation; for all the inner subconscious energies are then directed to the first stage, purification. The second stage, meditation, must come later when the job needed for the time being is done.

24

Fasting cannot guarantee against a return of any troubles which it succeeds in eliminating when their cause still remains uneliminated.

25

Although fasting will unquestionably contribute to purification of feelings and liberation from passions, it is not usually enough by itself to give more than temporary success; moreover it is beset with psychic dangers. Not all persons can undergo it safely. Yet it is worth consideration.

26

As the purificatory regime begins to show its effect, there will be clearly visible or strongly pronounced evidence of the stirring up and discharge of unpleasant impurities from the body through skin, bowels, urine, and mouth.

27

Fasting throughout its course and an unfired regime only in its early stages, eliminates so much waste toxins that bad breath appears as a symptom. However it can be greatly reduced by a combination of colon flushes and strong purges.

28

The cleansing effects of a fast follow only after the disturbing effects. For when the waste matter and excess mucous is stirred up (so that they can be carried away and thrown away), there results unpleasant physical symptoms and unhappy mental ones. But all this vanishes within two or three days in the case of long fasts, or certainly as soon as eating is resumed in the case of short ones.

29

The purifying process of an unfired diet works in the same way as that of a long fast. It does not make a single effort with a single result but rather a series of efforts with a series of results. Hence the distressing elimination symptoms are periodic and recurring, being successive and deepening stages of cleansing.

30

The inner urge in its favour is needed to sanction a fast; the instructive incentive must be felt before embarking on it. Otherwise, it will merely be forced starvation.

31

Everyone, except the persons whose physical constitution unfits them for it, should mark their entry upon the path of purification by a short fast. If he has never fasted before, it may be a modified fast during which he abstains from all solid food but takes well-diluted fruit or vegetable juices. Two to four days is sufficiently long for this purpose. Otherwise the best time to fast is at the opening of the seasons of spring and summer. Spring marks the beginning of the ancient new year, the real new year, around March 21. The more an aspirant purifies himself by using this simple method of physical fasting, the more will he be able to obtain a corresponding mental purification. After the first year or two, he will find it possible to go on to a fuller fast, during which nothing but water should be taken.

32

Gandhi was guided by his long experience with fasting to the firm belief that it tended to ascendancy of the mind over the body. He resorted to it whenever the spirit intuitively moved him to do so.

33

Interior stillness may emerge toward the latter part of a long fast. "Long" here must vary according to the individual—anything from four to twenty-four days. *A warning*: the older a person is the less can he endure a long fast; it is a matter of diminished resistance, and he courts death if he ignores this warning.

34

A series of short fasts, which may be from one to seven days each set at intervals of not less than twice their own length in the case of the longer ones and six times in that of the shortest ones, will be the safest way for most people.

35

Fasting throws the mind into a negative state which opens it to the possibility of mediumistic control. This is a risk which develops only after the third day and therefore longer fasts should be the exception rather than the rule.

36

Buddha, in the days of his intense search for truth, underwent a forty-nine day fast. But after his attainment of truth he consistently warned his followers against emulating his example. He explained that such long severe fasts were unnecessary torment of the body and that they did not bring one nearer the goal.

37

The factors which must determine the length of a fast are: the man's surrounding circumstances and physical strength, how much willpower he has, and what it is that he wishes to achieve or cure by the fast.

38

No fast ought to be for a longer period than one week unless it is borne by a well-experienced person with a well-balanced mind, or unless it is supervised by an authoritative experienced fasting expert.

39

Pythagoras required candidates to undergo a forty-day fast before he initiated them into his secret teachings. He said only so could their brains be sufficiently purified to understand such deep doctrine. A few fasts of two to four days in length will cause the average stomach distended by the long custom of overeating to shrink to its right proportions. If this lead, given by Nature, is henceforward followed, he will eat less than before but enjoy equal or more strength than before.

40

The traditionally prescribed Jain fast consists in abstinence from food and sometimes from water for thirty-six hours. It begins just after sunset and is broken after sunrise or later. It is performed on holy days, which are devoted to self-examination, self-criticism, and self-purification.

41

A partial liquid fast on vegetable water or fruit juice or lemonade is easier than an absolute one, while a restricted diet is easier than a partial fast.

42

It is not only the presence of excessive waste solids in the body that calls for purification but also the presence of excessive slimy mucous. It usually passes out after a fast, which shrivels the body and thus contracts the tissues until the mucous is forced out of its lodging places. The process is helped by drinking warm water with one-half teaspoon of lemon or lime juice and one-half teaspoon of honey in it. This loosens and thins the slime.

43

The Arab mystics practise a form of semi-fasting during their forty-day retreat into complete solitude for special meditation practice. Each day they eat no more than about a half loaf of bread and a dozen figs.

44

On fasts of three or four or more days, it is quite practicable—despite erroneous popular belief—to drink nothing, not even water, for the first day and thus give the kidneys a thorough rest. This obviously applies only to healing, not to cleansing fasts.

45

It is foolish to take a full meal when bringing a fast to an end. The digestive organ needs time to re-adjust itself. It is wiser to break the fast with liquid nourishment; go on to semi-solid and then only to solid food, by degrees.

46

It is best to make the first meal after a short fast on clear broth and the second meal on stewed prunes without sugar. Eat plenty as roughage is needed to clean waste out of the intestinal tract. The prunes give a laxative effect as well as needed fibrous roughage.

47

To break a fast, use warm water with a little mildly acidic fruit or fruit juice—lemon or tomato. Reserve the sweet fruits—oranges, grapes, and coconut water—for the second breaking of the fast. If possible use only distilled water for these drinks.

48

The work of purifying the body cannot be done sufficiently by fasting alone, or by diet alone, or by postural exercises alone, or by any other physical means alone. Each may be important, one may be more important to one individual than the others, but it is a combination of two or several that is needed.

49

So much of this noxious material is eliminated through the skin that three processes of cleansing are needed to counteract it. First, the warm bath. Many persons are not tough enough to stand the weakening effects of a too hot bath. It is better to be prudent and be satisfied with a moderately warm one. Second, the friction rub. Third, the frequent change of underclothing. It is a physiological fact that a part of this material can be re-absorbed into the body if these processes are neglected. When that happens, this rancid and poisonous stuff will open the way to disease.

50

The friction rub may be done with a small coarse rough face cloth or with a loofah sponge. The entire body should be vigorously scrubbed, but especially the feet. A cool—not cold—shower at the end will close the pores and stimulate circulation.

51

Among the Ojibwa Indians of North America there existed formerly an esoteric group of shamans who alone refused to become converted to the missionary type of Christianity. They studied the higher teachings of spiritual existence, which were reserved strictly to themselves. The ceremony of initiating a new member was *preceded* by sweat baths.

52

I have often quoted in talks Anatole France's terse brilliant phrase, "All is opinion." The Brahmins consider a twice-daily shower bath to be an essential part of their religion. The moderns say that cleanliness is next to godliness. Yet many a medieval monk remained unwashed for long periods, rejecting baths as luxuries for the effete and indulgences for the body.

53

Yogis consider that *basti*, the washing of the bowel, is the most essential of their cleansing procedures. This is essentially the same as our Western enema and colon-flushing procedures.

54

The squatting position is the natural one in which to answer a bowel movement call. It is the best one hygienically, too.

55

It is advisable to keep the breathing passages clear from mucous, especially the thick, gummy kind which adheres to the membranes. This can be done by gargling the throat and washing the nostrils by strongly breathing some water up the nasal passages, water which has been very slightly dissolved with salt and which is comfortably hot.

56

I suffer from mucous and have experimented with various remedies, but I found that the one thing which was most successful was to prevent its appearance altogether by wrapping a scarf twice round my throat and keeping it there.

57

If the eye muscles are overworked by too much desk work, regular resting at intervals during this work will enable them to recuperate their strength and efficiency. In this connection remember the advice given by my oculist that when using any eye drop medicine take care not to touch the eyes themselves with the eye cup or the dropper used. If one eye gets infected with, say, conjunctivitis in this way one avoids passing the infection to the other eye. The same care should be used with the small towel used for wiping the eyes after washing. Separate towels reserved for this purpose should be used or rather separate face cloths.

58

An eye specialist informs me that the blurring of sight which sometimes happens with the fall of darkness can be avoided by wearing red spectacles for a few minutes and avoiding looking directly at white light. He also advised me to trim odd eyelash hairs which got too long and irritated the eyeball and to do this regularly.

59

According to Dr. Aschner:

1. The three-week fast gives very good results in anti-arthritic treatment, especially where fingers are involved—swollen, stiff, etc. A little stale bread and a cup of prune juice is allowed per day. Heavy blankets on a sheet-wrapped body to produce perspiration are used at night.

2. Chronic indigestion through hyperacidity is treated by bitter tonic herbs—alkalizers are not enough. The best are gentian on empty stomach, vermouth, cinchona.

3. Breakfast: Fruit juices create heartburn; ban them; cereals slow digestion; toast is better. Boiled rice is easiest to digest.

60

Artificial and synthetic materials are preferably not to be worn next to the skin. Their use should be limited to outer and overgarments, which should be made, in that case, of mixed materials, so that nature's cotton or wool introduces its energies and less fatigue is induced.

61

They blindly obey, in their ways of living and eating, the suggestions received from their own lower nature, from their family, and from the world generally.

62

The break with long-held bad personal habits, coupled with the bringing to birth of entirely new good ones, is a difficult experience. But it is also an immensely rewarding one.

63

Essay: The Practical Technique of Fasting

The beginner should experiment with an eighteen hour fast, repeated every week or two weeks; extend it to twenty-four hour periods in a month or two, and later on to thirty-six or forty-eight hours at a stretch. Having thus well prepared himself, he should finish the regime with a single three, or three and a half day fast.

The fast starts in the evening by missing the dinner meal, and by taking instead, to help to empty the bowels completely, a mild dose of warm senna leaf infusion—a herbal laxative tea.

The next morning, take a cupful of mild herbal stomach cleanser, an infusion of Golden Seal herbs in warm water (also known commercially as Fluid Extract of Hydrastis). Follow this a half hour later by drinking a cupful of warm or hot water. This process is to be repeated on the last morning of the fast, if the latter extends to a three day period. Fasting should be preceded and ended by these purges.

At night, after the first complete day's fast, take an enema. Use warm, slightly soapy water (vegetable oil soap is essential), hold it within the body for as long as possible while lying flat for a minute or two. Turn over on the left side for a further minute or two and then turn over on the right side for the same period. Repeat on last night if fasting for three days. On each morning, take a warm bath, not exceeding five minutes and using soap. In the morning when dressing and in the early evening, use a tongue scraper. These long, thin, narrow strips, made of lightweight plastic, are stocked by most drugstores.

It is recommended that only distilled water be drunk and that the herbal infusions be made with that also. It can be bought in jars from better food or drugstores.

As an alternative to the full fast, you may conserve your strength for work by engaging in semi-fasts of the same duration as the full fast. During these periods eat no solid food and subsist on fruit juices well diluted with water, or else, on lemonade containing one-half teaspoon of raw honey to each tumbler of distilled water, or on vegetable extract water made by soaking diced carrot, celery, and parsley for five or six hours in distilled water, then straining off and discarding the solids. This drink may be mixed with the lemonade drink already described to render it more palatable if desired. Since, when unmixed, it contains no significant quantity of proteins and no starches, it belongs more closely to the category of full rather than semi-fast and may enable them to be better borne.

While fasting, do not exercise the body or undertake physically strenuous tasks. If you are working, it is advisable to carry out the fast during a weekend. It offers a convenient time to catch up on reading and meditation assignments. Experience demonstrates conclusively that if this period is spent sitting on a chair, reclining on a couch, or resting in a bed, it is passed through more easily, more swiftly, and more effortlessly, whereas, if spent active and moving about it is passed through with difficulty, slowly dragged out. So do not spend more than the least possible energy. Pray for guidance in self-improvement and for help in self-purification.

Headaches and fatigue often appear during the first and second days of fasting. They usually disappear along with hunger during the third day.

To end the fast, be careful to break it gently and by degrees. This preconditions the stomach for normal eating. It is a serious and sometimes a dangerous mistake to break a fast with solid food. The longer the fast, the more dangerous it is to do so. The correct way is to take a mild dose of warm liquid herbal laxative like senna leaves and wait for half an hour. Then, take liquid refreshment only—a warm, clear, vegetable soup containing no solids is best. The broth should be unspiced and unsalted. It should be made from one-third part at least of carrots and the remainder of mixed seasonal vegetables in which spinach predominates. Potatoes, being very starchy, must not be a part of it. The next meal may be a thick, heavy vegetable soup of which diced carrots are a substantial part. No dried beans or lentils may be included. For the first ordinary solid meal, avoid sharp, hard, crisp foods such as toast, as these can damage the temporarily tender stomach lining; avoid also such heavy, clogging starches as potatoes—as these retard the recovery of digestive activity.

The beneficial effect of fasting is both psychological and physical. Not only are the toxic matters eliminated but so also are obstructive waste matters and sticky slimes. This purification of the body lets it function more freely.

Although fasting is given a temporary place in the philosophic discipline because of its benefits, warning must be given of the possible injuries if it is practised without discrimination. If prolonged beyond the capacity of the body to endure, fasting may end in coma or sometimes even in death. The correct length of a fasting period depends partly upon the vitality and weight of the individual. Weak and thin persons cannot endure so long a one as strong or fat persons can. The period following any fast must not be regarded as unimportant. The body, being weakened, will not be able to endure strains that it can ordinarily endure; therefore, rest must be continued and only slowly discontinued. Take particular care not to lift heavy weights. Since pulsation of the heart and blood pressure are noticeably reduced by fasting, those persons who have an already low blood pressure and even those who are older than fifty years, should take care to avoid either a total fast or a long one. The dizziness which is felt by some fasters when they get up from lying in a bed or reclining on a couch can be lessened or prevented if they will be careful, when rising from this position, to move very slowly.

The physical dangers can be adequately safeguarded against by taking the precautions mentioned in the previous paragraph and by setting three and a half days as the maximum period for any one fast. It is harmful *not* to take a mild laxative just at the beginning of the fast as at the end, for the bowel motions stop and previous accumulations, having no intake of food to move them, remain clogged and constipating. But those who use strong mineral salts—which heat the membrane lining the stomach rendered delicate by the fast—when mild herbal ones are available are ill-advised.

The psychical dangers also do not usually arise except on fasts extended for periods longer than this time. The chief one is the negative condition of mediumship, which opens the mind to the influence of other persons and the body to control by disincarnate entities. *No aspirant who already shows mediumistic tendencies should practise fasting for longer than one or two days at a time. The sick and the old must take all needed precautions, modify the fast to suit their individual condition, or adopt the semi-fast. Sufferers from serious lung or heart disease must not attempt any form of fasting.*

A series of intermittent fasts with one week between the twenty-four hour fast or two weeks between the two, three, or four day ones are preferable to very long abstinences. They are less drastic, much safer, and not less efficacious at the end of a course. The end of a course in fasting should be followed by a reformed diet. It is much less difficult after such a course to drop from one's diet any article of food or drink of which one has been fond for many years and to which one has been so addicted that its absence would be highly disturbing. The same is true of adding any new dietary articles which may seen unattractive and unpalatable. This fact makes the fast an easier and useful way of making the transition from wrong eating habits to better ones.

It is inadvisable to fast in winter as the cold weather is easily felt. The best times are spring, summer, and early autumn. Especially suitable times are:

(a) at the two equinoxes, March 21 when the sun crosses the equator on its northward journey and thus inaugurates the spring season, and about September 23 when it again crosses the equator on its southward journey and inaugurates the autumn season.

(b) at the summer solstice, when the sun changes its course and reverses its direction. This happens about June 21.

At these three dates, Nature is preparing her great cyclic changes throughout the world and in Man. It is then that the cleansing of man's body prepares him for these changes.

5

EXERCISE

The body has to be rendered fit by a course of purification and training in posture to practise meditation. It is not *ordinarily* ready to do so without such previous preparation, geniuses excepted. The posture training is of two kinds. First, the spine and head must be straightened by a slight contraction of the anus, a pull of the navel region backwards and upwards, a drawing-up of the neck and head. There are psychic and energy currents from the solar plexus passing up the spine during meditation to the brain. Not only is their free movement hindered by a bent body or a sunken chest, but they are unable to attain their proper strength. The second kind of posture training is to find the fixed position in which one can sit steadily for a long time without getting uncomfortable. This is necessary because if the body is moving about, or working, or shaking, the mind cannot attain the proper depth of thought or subtlety of attention or absorption needed for meditation, nor can the collection and concentration of the vital forces needed for the same purpose occur.

2

We are so tied to the foolish idea which regards body and mind as two wholly separate and different entities, that all too many regard it as undignified to practise physical exercises in order to influence the mind. The discoveries of mentalism show how foolish is such an attitude, how much we miss in outer helps to inner attainment.

3

Less than two centuries ago most men were working on the land, the sea, and the forests and mines. In the cities they worked in hand-operated workshops and the cities themselves were not so large; the countryside was close at hand. They worked hard and long, using the muscles of their bodies, and so did their wives. This involuntary exercise of the muscular system, this exposure to sunshine and fresh air, this limitation to fresh and unpreserved foods, kept most of them healthy and strong even if the lack of better housing and sanitation kept short the lives of some of them. Then came the industrial revolution, when the machine and the civilization it created changed their habits of living. Now they crowd into cities, enter sedentary occupations, sit in chairs for long hours, or stand at mechanical assembly lines. Their bodies become soft, flabby, and undeveloped. Their organs of digestion function imperfectly. Yet such is their hypnotized condition that they do not often realize the harm which modern ways have done them; indeed, they usually pity their ancestors! But those who do realize it and feel uneasy in their conscience about it, need to make a positive effort to eliminate the deterioration and the atrophy which are the price paid for straying away from Nature.

4

There is no better way to bring the body under control than the way used to bring the mind under control—to put it under a daily routine of exercises and to have a fixed time for their repeated practice.

5

The best time naturally to do exercises is on rising from bed, but it may not be the most convenient time.

6

If the body is a battery and needs regular recharging (through relaxation practices), it is also a structure and needs reconditioning (through indicated exercises.)

7

Cicero's prescription to follow the daily period of exercise with a period of rest is an excellent one.

8

It is possible with only twelve months of regular, daily work to build up a perfect physical control.

9

The ordinary bodily exercises can soon become tiring to middle-aged people. Moreover they take twice or treble the time needed for the simple culture of the spine, which is the most concentrated form of exercise possible. It stretches the body to the limit.

10

It may be too much to ask students who have reached middle or old age to try all these exercises in physical betterment or follow all these instructions in physical coordination. But what they may find impossible to perform or what they may be disinclined to practise, they can still make advantageous use of in the following way. Let them bring such teaching to the notice of younger persons, to children in their teens and those just beyond the threshold of adulthood—for it is far easier for these younger persons to do than for older ones. The effort required is much less, the habits not so much encrusted.

11

The body is deliberately made to exercise itself in certain attitudes and gestures. Any gesture becomes an attitude when it is arrested.

12

Care of the physical organism will require attention to physical exercise as well as physical relaxation and to deep and abdominal breathing.

13

The disuse of some muscles and the misuse of others can only lead to bodily faults. Restore the first to use, correct the second.

14

If any exercise has unpleasant effects such as discomfort or pain, its practice should be discarded for a time. The cause should be sought for and, if found, remedied. There may be a mistake in the manner in which the exercise is done.

15

It is not necessary to practise vigorous exercises that quickly tire one, nor to put forth strenuous exertions that make one perspire. There are mild, simple, and slow movements which can bring about the desired results without them.

16

The custom of working earnestly at self-improvement through a series of exercises done every day, exercises which involve the body as well as the mind, is somewhat frightening to lazy people, somewhat impracticable to busy people, and somewhat superhuman to average ones. This is why so many of those who start any regime of regular exercises fail to continue and finish the course. The longer the daily period required, the sooner their enthusiasm wanes. Only those succeed who have exceptional determination and unusual persistence. The fact is, we are not easily amenable to rigorous discipline. But if the period of daily work were limited to essentials for a few minutes only, many more people would remain faithful to it.

17

The idea of doing exercises for a space of time daily carries a suggestion of monotony and boredom with it.

18

The value of stretching and bending exercises is twofold. First, there is the local and beneficial effect on the particular part of the body's muscles and organs. Second, there is the general good effect which comes from the deep breathing they induce.

19

The greatest benefit is got by bending the entire trunk, which means bending forwards, backward, and sideways.

20

When a muscle is regularly compelled to undergo a series of stretches and contractions, not only is it kept flexible but it is also kept strong.

21

By working a muscle group against resistance, he will build up will-power as well as muscle power.

22

Holding the spine properly allows the flow currents of this Spirit-Energy to circulate properly.

23

The benefit of a specific exercise is to be measured by the warmth, or kundalini, it creates—not by the time it takes.

24

Those who have seldom or never done bodily exercises may find it hard to start or, if started, to finish the complete daily period. It would be a pity if they gave up before sufficient time had passed to feel the benefits of the work.

25

Merely to lie down reduces the heartbeats by no less than ten each minute, thus saving this ever-working organ some of its heavy labour.

26

The simple exercise of stretching helps to counter the congestions, compressions, and adhesions which obstruct the flow of the vital force through the spinal column with its sixty-two branching nerves and thus to regain energy. This truth of the need of spine-loosening movement is instinctively known by every dog and cat, every lion and tiger, for they apply it immediately after awakening from sleep. The back, the legs, and even paws are bent and stretched and even rolled by them in this natural exercise.

27

(a) To make the spinal column flexible and serviceable for these purposes, it must be both loosened and stretched. The exercise which can do this is to stand with arms straight overhead and feet pointing to the front. Turn the upper trunk above the waist as far to the right as possible, repeat to the left. Breathe in deeply, hold breath and grasp an imaginary parallel bar with the two hands before making these movements, and pull yourself upward during them. An incidental effect of this exercise is to invigorate and stimulate the general tone of the body.

(b) The top of the spine and the neck area surrounding it need a supplementary exercise to complete the work. This simply consists of drawing the chin slightly inward and then giving an upward pull to the head and neck; then when this series is finished, half turn the head to the right, later to the left. All these simple semi-rotations of the upper body take little time but give a large result.

28

By drawing up the whole body as straight and as tall as it will go—a process which consciously uses, stretches, and strengthens the muscles—the spine is held erect and the head high. This simple exercise gives grace to the form, vitality to its movements, and resistance to sickness.

29

Ruth Revere offered an exercise to iron out the curves of the spine, strengthen the muscles around the spinal vertebrae, and integrate the pelvis with the spine for firm support in the upright position. It involves lying on your back on the mat or rug. Bend your knees up over your body. Clasp the tips of your fingers around your knees. Round your elbows and ease your shoulders. Now, with the right knee in line with the right shoulder and the left knee in line with the left shoulder, rock your whole body slowly from side to side. Go as far as you can without flopping or resting your elbows on the floor. Keep your arms round. Start to the other side by using your inner, centering muscles (abdomen). This forces you to straighten out your spine with every effort. In time you will get the feel of it and every attempt will help. It relaxes the back muscles.

30

The spinal column stores nerve force and delivers it to all the nerve-endings which terminate in it. These nerves carry this force throughout the body. Since this includes the brain, we may see how important it is to take proper care of the spine. There are three ways to do so: posture, exercise, and stimulation. The first requires us to carry the spinal column erect. The second is to turn, bend, and twist it daily so as to keep it supple. The third is to stimulate it by cold showers or wet packs. Take wet towels alternately hot and cold, fold them over until they are about four inches wide, and lay them on the back along the whole length of the spine. The water in which the towels are dipped should be alternately as hot and as cold as one can bear without discomfort.

31

Many persons are not hardy enough to withstand the shock of a very cold shower. Those who are not physically strong enough to endure it should be satisfied with a cool one; otherwise the kidneys, the heart, or the bladder may be injured.

32

The total training and balanced endeavour of philosophy are enough by themselves to avoid any danger from identification with the body. But it takes an additional precaution against it by introducing the following declaration for momentary practice during the pauses between different movements or positions: "I am not this limited body. It is my servant. I am infinite Mind."

33

That good posture is one of the determinants of a purified body may seem too bold an assertion to be credible even to many who may be able to grant that it is one of the determinants of physical fitness. Let them remember that the spine is the trunk of a tree, the central nerve system, crowned by the brain, the organ of thought.

34

The connections between the neck, the thorax, and the breathing process must be understood and brought under conscious control.

35

A proper self-respect will of itself straighten the posture and remove the sag in the middle. But the opposite is just as true. A proper posture will add self-respect to the character.

36

The poise of the head, the posture of the spine, and the functioning of the breath determine every attitude of the whole body.

37

By lowering the centre of the body's gravity in all its activities, whether sitting, walking, or standing, we are raising its ability to obey the will and the mind.

38

Proper posture does not mean stiff posture.

39

The basic principle taught by yoga in this connection is that the back should be carried as erect as possible. As it is ordinarily and unconsciously carried, the vertebrae are pressed together so that the spinal column is actually shortened. But as it ought to be carried, they should be pulled away from each other so that the spinal column is actually lengthened.

40

There is a common idea, probably derived from now outdated military drills, that right posture involves lifting up and throwing back the shoulders and stiffening the knees. This is wrong as it throws too much strain on the body and fatigues the nerves.

41

What the head initiates, the remainder of the body follows. This, in the case of the developed man, is true of what lies inside the head. But concerning the physical head itself, it is true of all men, developed and undeveloped.

42

The relation of consciousness to the ego expresses itself in the use of the ego. The use expresses itself in the relation between the head and the trunk.

43

Beware of the student's stoop.

44

The writer whose head is drooped and whose neck is bent by desk work is not in the best posture to generate inspired ideas.

45

This training of the spine has some valuable secondary and incidental results. Although these are connected with the improvement of health and eradication of disease, and as such are not the direct object of the training, their value remains a great one for sufferers. For instance, weak and painful backs can be the result of several different causes but one of them is faulty posture when walking. The following way of carrying the torso is bad: drawing the shoulders and chest too far back and pushing the abdomen too far forward. This curves the spine in the wrong direction and unnecessarily throws too much weight upon it.

46

Fatigue may allow the spine to sag, thus flattening the cushion-like cartilages between its discs and impinging on the nerve branches. This in turn restricts the inflow of nerve force and lowers nerve energies.

47

The spine is so delicately built up that it is affected for the worse by the soft beds in which the body sleeps for several hours nightly. A harder surfaced bed is better for it.

48

It is not a necessary accompaniment of spirituality that a man be weak and sickly in body.

49

Those who suffer from spinal troubles or hip diseases should not practise any physical exercises without previous permission from their physician.

50

Between the two extreme forms of exaggerated posture, the slouch and the soldier, the first of course is the more serious.

51

Even when attending to the ordinary duties of every day routine, if this is done by throwing more work upon particular muscles than they need do, albeit unconsciously, then it is done badly. The end result is fatigue.

52

Entering a room, going to a chair, or walking in a street should not be done by a soul-guided man too quickly or too violently. It is ungraceful and unspiritual in appearance, while disturbing mentally. Gentle, leisurely movements are more suitable.

53

If you study the walking habits of men who have attained this tranquillity, you will find that slowness of movement accompanies sacredness of quality.

54

The nuns are taught not to rush across a room nor to run along a corridor. A paced, slowed walk is the proper way. This helps recollection, remembrance, self-control, and a growth of inner calm.

55

Even his bodily movements must be brought into conformity with his mental attitude. His very gait in walking must be brought frequently to conscious attention and harmonized with the deliberations, the patience, the equilibrium, and the uprightness which, ideally, exist there.

56

When we remember that so much of the day we are doing these very things—sitting, standing, walking, breathing, resting, or sleeping—the importance of doing them in the right way may be realized. They are functions which may easily be done in the wrong way, and continue so for years, and even for a whole lifetime.

57

Whether it be to practise meditation or to fall and lie asleep, the position of the body should be such as to prevent it from becoming cramped or taut.

58

Shall the mystic walk with anaemic face and flat feet through life and let only the materialist walk with forceful step and resolute mien?

59

Western physical exercises seem designed to create bulging muscles, an over-expanded chest, and special athletic skills. It is enough for the healthful development of a balanced human being to bring the muscles no farther than the point of easy and instant obedience, to make the body perform its varied functions adequately and gracefully.

60

Whereas Western gymnastic exercises are intended to develop muscle, Eastern exercises are intended to develop control.

61

All physical techniques have an indirect helpfulness but their value should not be overrated, as the advocates and teachers of these techniques almost always do. They misplace their emphasis on the body and on the tricks it is able to perform. Only one detail of the human organism deserves their greater emphasis and that is intuition.

62

The Occidental worship of bodily arts, cultures, sports, exercises, and regimes would be excellent if it were part of a larger program of living that included the spiritual. But it is not. The Occidental mostly stops and ends with glorification of the body.

63

There is a most important difference between the work done in ordinary physical culture and the work done in this system. Those who jump about on a gymnasium floor or lift weights or engage in outdoor sports do so usually for the body's sake. But students who follow philosophic teachings practise their exercises for the Quest's sake. This fully respects the body and cares scrupulously for it.

64

It would be a delusion to believe that the practice of these physical disciplines alone can bring enlightenment. It is not obtainable by stretching the body, or holding the breath, although these may quite indirectly help to prepare the way for obtaining it. The ego must be transcended.

65

It is as necessary to make a daily ritual of these cleansing habits and physical exercises as it is of religious or mystical ones. They should be combined, the physical being practised *before* the spiritual ritual as a preparation for it and for the day's activity.

66

Tai Chi is a system of slow, gentle, graceful movements combined with meditation. It can be used either for self-defense, health, or aesthetics. Breath control is a vital element of this practice. Weight and pressure are made to sink down to what is called in Zen the Hara Centre (near the solar plexus). This system belongs to Chinese Taoism.

67

Long ago the dervishes in the Near East used a system of training which gave extraordinary control over the muscular system, swift reflexes, and striking mental concentration. For example, they would direct the movements of one limb while at the same time they directed another limb in a different way.

68

Too much exercise may be as harmful in the end as too little, while improper exercise may be more injurious than either.

69

Posture exercises: (1) Stand with feet together. Pinch buttocks together. Hold for five counts; relax. (2) Stretching neck straight up, automatically pulls stomach in. Stretch—using, for example, a cool radiator as a ballet dancer's bar—legs and torso.

70

Those who show their impatience by constantly tapping with their fingers or who betray their nervousness by fidgeting with their feet would benefit by a course in hatha yoga.

71

All such exercises are prohibited to anyone suffering from high blood pressure.

72

We do not deny but on the contrary fully accept the ingenuity and effectiveness of hatha yoga methods. They are cleverly designed to achieve their particular aims and are capable of doing so. But what we do deny is first, their suitability for modern Western man and second, their safety for modern Western man. And we make these denials both on the ground of theory and on the ground of practice. These methods are extremely ancient; they are indeed remnants of Atlantean systems. The mentality and physique of the races for whom they were originally prescribed are not the same as the mentality and physique of the white Euramerican races. Evolution has been actively at work during the thousands of years between the appearance of the ancients and the appearance of the moderns. Important changes have developed in the nerve-structure and brain-formations of the human species. According to the old texts which have come down to us from a dateless antiquity, the trance state constitutes the pinnacle of hatha yoga attainment. But it is an entirely unconscious kind of trance. This we have learnt from the lips of hatha yogis who had perfected themselves in the system. It is indeed nothing more mentally than an extremely deep sleep brought on deliberately and at will, although physically it bestows extraordinary properties for the time being on the body itself. Even where the trance is so prolonged that the yogi may be buried alive under earth without food or drink for several days or weeks, he is throughout that period quite inactive mentally and quite unaware of his own self. His heartbeat and respiration are then extremely low, in fact imperceptible to human senses although perceptible to delicate electric instruments like the cardiogram.

In what way does this condition differ from the animal hibernation? In northern climates certain types of reptiles, rodents, bears, lizards, marmots, and bats retire to secluded places, mountain caves or sheltered holes under the ground, when the cold weather arrives and when food becomes scarce, and pass the whole winter in a state of deep-sleeping suspended animation. In tropical climates certain kinds of snakes and crocodiles do exactly the same when the hottest months arrive. It is particularly interesting to note that birds like the tinamou fall into a rigid cataleptic trance under the shock of terror and then become as immune to pain as the hatha yogis do in the same state. In both cases there is only a hypnotic and not a spiritual condition. Its value for mental enlightenment, let alone moral improvement, is nil.

Twentieth-century man has better things to do with his time and energy than to spend several years and arduous efforts merely to imitate these animals and birds. Such a trance benefits the animals who cannot get food and it is therefore sensible procedure for them to enter it. But how does man demonstrate his spiritual superiority over them if he follows the bat to its cave in the hills, lets the same torpor creep over him as creeps over it, and permits every conscious faculty to pass into a coma? In terms of consciousness, of spiritual advance, the hatha yoga hibernation has nothing to offer man in any way comparable with what the higher systems of yoga have to offer—unless of course he disdains the fruits of mental evolution and takes pleasure in atavistic reversion to the state of these wide-winged yogis, the bats, and those four-footed mystics, the rodents! We should therefore remember that there are different types of trance state and should seek only the higher ones, if we wish to make a real rather than illusory progress.(P)

73

Choose those exercises which come easiest to you. You will have to do them every day.

74

Body purification and strengthening are prerequisites and preparations for spiritual awakening and development. They allow the passage of kundalini and also awaken it. Hence, hatha yoga is prescribed to start with.

75

The practice of any physical yoga posture will necessarily be difficult in its early stages because it throws the body into unfamiliar and unaccustomed positions. The muscles need to be re-educated little by little. It is dangerous to try to force oneself into such a posture all at once. Therefore, the exercise should be done for a few seconds only at the beginning, and the period extended by a few more seconds after several days, and further extended after a few weeks. In any case, it must be followed by a rest period before being repeated.

76

In ancient times when those who pursued yoga practices usually retired to peaceful forests and rugged mountains, lived simple disciplined lives, ate less rather than more, took little or no flesh food, and kept closer to Nature than their modern prototypes, the hindrance of ill-health was less frequent than nowadays. In their secluded settlements, they were often out of reach both of professional medical help and professionally prescribed medicines—so they usually learnt to depend on wild-growing herbs as far as these were available, and on applications of intense pressure applied to diseased parts of the body or to the breathing process. The healing herbs are Nature's gift to man and many of them have indeed been incorporated in the pharmacopoeia used by modern Western scientific medicine but more wait to be added. The pressures have possibilities of being equally efficacious but, like a double-edged sword, constitute at one and the same time an instrument of some power and some danger. We have seen both striking cures and terrible disasters follow the practice of these physical yoga exercises when done without the careful personal supervision of a trained teacher and in several cases even when this supervision was available. Our final conclusion is that it is not enough to have a teacher who merely knows how to do them. It is really necessary to have during the earlier attempts the watchful supervision or veto of a qualified medical man who understands the anatomical dangers and physiological changes involved.

77

The purpose of assuming such an unusual posture as that depicted in Buddha statues is manifold. One of them is to make such an abrupt break from the habits and postures of everyday ordinary life that the world, its cares and difficulties and temptations, is more easily forgotten.

78

These hatha yoga exercises seem to involve unnatural distortions and unnecessary struggles. Why should we contort the body and assume disagreeable postures which merely copy the forms of lower animals and reptiles like the tortoise, the cobra, and fish? Why should we, as human beings, so degrade ourselves and submit to these indignities? Are the benefits of these exercises real or alleged ones?

79

The artist, the thinker, or the mystic must not neglect the muscular vigour and health of body that can be obtained through physical yoga. This would include deep breathing, stretching exercises, and a diet of light and easily digested foods which will not dull inspiration.

80

If hatha yoga remains only a matter of muscle and sinew and breath, then the practitioner has touched only the surface of yoga.

81

When the hatha yogi continues a single practice for an abnormally long period, a change takes place in the pressure and the circulation of his blood stream. The fixed holding of breath, the fixed posture, the fixed gaze—any of these may bring it about. Spiritually, it has no more value than a fainting swoon and leads to no more illumination or happiness than that does.

82

Philosophical training puts much value on the quality of mental calmness, emotional composure, and on its reflected state in the body—physical stillness. The more a man's mind is self-composed, the more will his whole personality be self-possessed. The passions of hatred, greed, lust, and anger cannot then blind him to the truth about his human situation or about the world's nature. The bodily postures prescribed by the yoga system of physical control serve their highest purpose, and fulfil their ultimate intention, when they train a man in the art of being perfectly still. For such a man will gradually transfer some of the body's outer quietude to the mind's inner stillness. But he will do so only if properly instructed by book or teacher or correctly guided from within.

83

The *Shavasaha* or "Dead" posture is most useful. It is practised on the floor or on a stiff mattress. The arms are stretched, the palms face upward, and the feet are kept apart. Focus attention on the inhalation and exhalation of breath and shut the eyes. Held for ten to twenty minutes, this posture relaxes the entire body and removes fatigue.

84

The yogis assume the Buddha posture not only to save themselves from a fall should they slip into the trance state, but also should they inadvertently enter the ordinary sleep state. It is to prevent the drowsiness which develops into sleep that they sit stiffly erect. These are all surface reasons; there are deeper ones, which refer to Spirit-Energy.

85

The lotus posture draws much blood away from the feet and draws more blood into the brain. This helps the concentration of thought.

86

According to the classic yoga tradition, such a position must be steadily maintained without a change and indeed without a movement. Once the aspirant has found ease and comfort in a posture, subject to the rules already explained, he must establish himself in it and remain there.

87

All hatha yoga exercises are most conveniently done by spreading a rug, a carpet, or blanket on a clean floor.

88

Hatha yoga breathing exercises: The deep breath is drawn in suddenly, violently, and noisily, and then held. The spine is straightened up when inhaling.

89

There are several different traditional crossed-hand positions from which to choose to complete the crossed-leg posture: (a) the left hand may be placed on the right thigh and the right hand on the left thigh; (b) the left wrist may be crossed diagonally over the right wrist, both resting between the knees; (c) the left hand, palm upward, may be placed inside the right palm; (d) the left hand may clasp the right one as if shaking hands; (e) each hand may cross the breast and rest on the opposite shoulder; (f) both hands may rest together in—and be supported by—the lap, the left palm inside the right one, both vertically upright.

90

The refusal to study hatha yoga is short-sighted, narrow-minded, and unjustified, for this—as the yoga of body control—lays some foundation for the mental and higher yogas. Hatha yoga is not concerned only with gaining abnormal physical power as the opponents seem to believe, but also with gaining physical health, freedom from sickness, abundant vitality, and especially a purified nervous system and disciplined instincts. The Indian government subsidizes an ashram for the scientific study of hatha yoga, not far from Bombay, because of the resultant physical benefits.

91

Hatha yoga can give lithe movements to the body without the long arduous hours of gymnasium practice, can bestow youthful elasticity to it without the violent labours of the amateur or professional athlete.

92

To the young, hatha yoga is a new system of acrobatics. To others who say, "I don't want the religious and philosophical side of yoga," it seems purely practical. The proper value of hatha yoga is as a preparation for the spiritual path. But how remote is all this posturing and sniffing, this preoccupation with physical exercises, from real spirituality!

93

Although most of hatha yoga's postures seem contorted, queer, and even dangerous, they have their merits and usefulness. The risks come in when one tries to do too much too soon.

94

Hatha yoga exercises practised at night give deeper, more refreshing sleep; also, one passes into sleep more quickly.

95

Hatha Yoga: These pressures were self-applied through forcing the body to assume a particular immobile posture for fixed periods of time. The steadiness which was maintained during such postures had a steadying effect on the consciousness, too, and so they were also adopted by healthy yogis, as an indirect means of attaining the requisite concentration, and ultimately, because of the effect on the interaction of heart and brain, the requisite inhibition of thinking. Thus, the yoga of body control has come to be traditionally handed down to the present day.

96

Hatha yoga operates on the physical body only, and only so far as it is an instrument useful for inner development. Its ultimate use is to awaken the Serpent-Power.

97

Physical yoga postures exercise pressure upon the psychic nerve centres.

98

According to the system of Patanjali, the aim of a yogi should be to stop all movement of the mind and body. Consequently he cannot but become a recluse if he is to follow this system completely.

99

That these disciplines, methods, and exercises have a preventive value as regards possible disease and a therapeutic value as regards actual disease is fully believed in the Orient.

100

There is another possible view of hatha yoga which is that so far as its severe distortions of the body impose actual pain upon it, the suffering cancels evil karma of the past. The exercises thus seen are a form of penance and self-mortification.

101

The twists and poses of the body which physical (hatha) yoga requires may empty the mind, if sustained at length, but cannot attract the Spirit. But the inner and outer rest they bring have a value in their own place.

102

If we look at some of the yogis who can perform these extraordinary feats, we find their muscles to be quite ordinary in development. This indicates that it is not the size of the muscle but the force put into it which is the real agent in making the feats possible.

103

In *A Hermit in the Himalayas*, I have told of those practisers of hatha yoga who held their breath too long and exploded a blood vessel in the lungs, causing serious injury. There are others, however, who have been luckier, for with them the exploded vessel is in the brain, but it has not gone far enough to cause a paralytic stroke. It has gone far enough, though, to disrupt those parts of the brain which concern past memory and future anticipation, so that the yogi is left with a consciousness dwelling only in the immediate moment. This is something like The Eternal Now sensed by the philosopher and gives the yogi a kind of peace, a freedom from cares and fears. He will then declare that he has entered *samadhi*, not understanding that he has become a case for medical attention. His physical movements will slow down to the point of uncertainty, his fellow yogis will admire his attainment and become his followers, and he will become a guru!

104

Are there difficulties and dangers for the Westerner in Indian yoga? The answer is that this is true of some kinds of yoga technique but not of all, and for many Westerners but not for all. I have come across many cases during my travels where aspirants have wrecked health or mind through plunging blindly into yoga, and this is equally true of Indians themselves. It has always been my endeavour to protect readers of my books by communicating only what I know to be safe methods. I have deliberately kept silent about the others. However, if the student keeps his feet on earth, if he does not renounce common sense and a balanced life, and if he stops practising if untoward signs should ever appear and consults an expert about them, there is really little to fear. Most of the people who have gone astray though yoga have been neurotics, fanatics, and the mildly insane.

105

The physical yoga teachers rarely possess a knowledge of physiology. They do not know the precise physiological effects of the breathing exercises and postures they prescribe upon muscles, organs, and bones. This is why some of their pupils come to serious injury.

106

Because everyone can see and touch a body whereas few can sense a mind, the teacher of a physical yoga method will find many more followers than other teachers do. But the results of following it will leave its practisers with as much egoism as they had before. In some cases, where unusual powers and tricks of the body can be displayed, it will leave them with even more egoism than before!

107

The danger of an excess of physical yoga—as of all physical culture—to a person who at the same time is practising meditation and seeking a subtler consciousness, lies in the loss of sensitivity caused by greater immersion in the body.

108

He must begin this work by accepting the tenet that he is not the body, only a tenant in the body. Otherwise he may fall into the danger that so many hatha yogins fall into: the inability to achieve mystical experience or practise metaphysical thinking.

109

The teachers and followers of the religious devotion, mental concentration, and metaphysical study schools generally condemn physical yoga. Does not this show that they are as biased against it as those who teach physical yoga are biased for it? Only an independent attitude can remove the unfairness of the one and the exaggeration of the other.

110

The yoga of body control has a distinct and useful place in human life and constitutes a valuable system of practice. But when we hear exaggerated claims on its behalf, then it is time to remind its intemperate advocates that no amount of standing on their head will ever bring them into the realization of God.

111

Consciousness of the Spirit is not obtained by contortion of the legs.

112

Tsong Khapa, in his younger days, mastered hatha yoga enough to gauge its real worth and place and then proceeded to the higher yogas which led him to fitness for his mission, which changed the history of Tibetan religion.

113

A modern Indian holy man, Shukacharya, of the Province of Gujerat, who died as recently as 1929 and who had thousands of followers who regarded him as a divine incarnation, told his disciples in one of his discourses: "Your Guru has practised all of the hatha yoga asanas for quite a long time and it is his definite verdict that it's all labour wasted, insofar as the ideal of self-realization is concerned. In fact, the human mind is the home of all maladies; it is vulnerable at each end and it is necessary to purge it of all diseases and to stitch all leakages; if it is so, where is the earthly sense in wrestling with the muscles? The primary concern, therefore, is to treat the mind and not the body."

114

We must keep a proper proportion in our minds between these different branches of self-preparation and purification. A man whose spine is straight but whose conduct is crooked is doing worse than a man whose conduct is straight but whose spine is crooked.

115

The physical regimes and disciplines of hatha yoga purify the body and restore health, but they are not sufficient to answer the mind's questionings, nor to still the heart's yearning for peace.

116

The hatha yogis are inclined to give too much importance to the practice of these bodily disciplines. When this happens they become obstacles on the way, new attachments that have to be broken.

117

Eugene Sandow, once the strongest man in Europe, confirms the point. He said, "It is a matter of the mind. If you concentrate your mind upon a set of muscles for three minutes a day, and say 'Do thus and so,' they respond."

118

The practices are not dull if the beneficial end results are kept in mind. And although they were originally designed for other purposes, they are all health-giving and some are therapeutic.

119

Another of the beneficial purposes of these fixed postures is that they sustain and maintain a bodily stillness. Those persons who are subject to fidgeting limbs, restless fingers, or twitching muscles are trained and disciplined by this practice to overcome the fault which left alone would make meditation impossible.

120

These stretching exercises tend to produce freer movements of the body by making the muscles more elastic, the joints looser, and the sinews less stiff. The spinal exercises tend to produce a fine, erect carriage which particularly improves the appearance of middle-aged persons or even older ones.

121

Although from the standpoint of the special psychic purpose of these exercises, their physical benefits are secondary and incidental, this does not make them less valuable. The aged, the studious, and the overworked particularly need these benefits of more vigour, more buoyancy, quicker response, and better functioning.

122

Instead of following the ordinary Western methods of carrying out certain movements of bodily parts which are designated "exercises," to improve the condition of those parts, this system uses fixed postures and muscular pressures, and even more, takes advantage of, and utilizes profitably, the ordinary movements by which everyone has to carry on daily activities.

123

These are exercises for people without the time and certainly without the inclination to become skilled gymnasts or tumbling acrobats. They are brief, simple, and convenient. No special apparatus is needed.

124

The orthodox kind of gymnasium exercise, with its long, violent exertions which tend to stiffen the muscles and tire the body, is unsuited to sedentary middle-aged persons. Its drudgery exhausts them whereas the philosophic exercise invigorates them.

125

Westerners tend to do these exercises too violently as they actually expect to do all those of their own systems.

126

Some of the exercises are artificial and violent because they are intended to bring about the greatest result in the shortest time. Others make use of natural movements and are not only intended to correct the errors which wrong habit has introduced into these movements, but also to let them, when they are perfectly done, assist in keeping the body fit and vital.

127

Some have tapped the power in these postures to kindle the body's own natural healing forces. This may happen if two conditions are provided. First, the posture must be assumed along with *inheld* breath. Second, it must be sustained for as long as possible without change. Third, the mind must be concentrated at the same time upon the bodily part affected and its perfect healthy condition inwardly "seen."

128

1. Draw the diaphragm inwards so as to hollow the body immediately under the ribs.

2. Then draw the diaphragm upwards, spreading out the chest.

3. This exercise must be accompanied by appropriate aspiration toward the ideal.

129

Here are two unusual exercises: (a) Sideways Walking, that is, extend the right leg to the side and draw the left one after it; then extend the left leg to the side and draw the right after it. (b) Backwards Walking. Both these movements use the body in a way it is quite unaccustomed to, and therefore develop another side of it.

130

Lie flat on the back, with the hands resting at the sides. Tense all the muscles throughout the body and press it against the floor as hard as you can. By drawing in the abdominal wall and contracting the abdominal muscles, the lower spine can be more flattened against the floor. Try to bring as much of your back in contact with the floor as possible. When tired, rest. Repeat the rhythm of pressure and rest five times. *Variation (a)* Perform the same exercise but raise both feet six inches in the air, still tensing their muscles. When tired, rest. Repeat three times. *Variation (b)* Sit on hard chair, hands on hips, feet flat on floor. Straighten the lower back curve by contracting the abdominal and gluteal muscles, the pelvis will then be held at the proper angle, the trunk will be at a right angle to the thighs. Then relax these muscles. These exercises invigorate the whole body in a very short time and force the breath to deepen itself. They straighten the lower back curve.

131

Where a parallel bar is not available, an alternate exercise can be substituted by lying flat and stretching spine and feet and toes to the utmost.

132

The length of the period of rest between the movements cannot be prescribed for general use. It must vary with each individual's varying strength. The sooner he tires, the longer should the rest period be. If a few seconds will suffice for one person, especially a younger person, a full half-minute may be needed by another, especially an older person.

133

He should inject his whole self into doing the exercise so completely that he is almost unaware of anything else at the time. Such mental concentration is one of the secrets of champion professional strongmen.

134

Except where specially instructed not to do so, take a short rest after every exercise to let breathing return to normal and sore muscles become comfortable, and only then repeat the movement.

135

The faithful practice of these mind-concentrated physical exercises must lead in time to better bodily self-control.

136

The order of procedure is: first stretch the body with one or two of the physical exercises, then cleanse and invigorate it with one or two of the breathing exercises, then sit in meditation.

137

It is the *combination* at one and the same practice time of exercise plus breathing plus concentrated thought which evokes the greatest power and brings about the greatest results.

138

He may practise meditation until Doomsday, mutter the hundred and eight different mystic spells, sit in all the sixty-four postures of the yoga of body control, hold his breath for a whole hour or vary its rhythms in every conceivable manner, but the Overself will remain stubbornly remote un-less he frankly faces and successfully fights out his struggle against his own ego in his own heart. No physical contortion, exercise, or manipulation can ever take its place. Such yoga exercises can discipline his body, give him control over it, but they cannot provide a passport into the higher region. This and this alone is the only yoga that really counts in the end on this strange quest, because demanding all it gives all.

139

It is not necessary to give more than a little time to these exercises, not more than is necessary to keep the body reasonably strong and fit.

140

Those who have any part or organ of the body in a defective or weakened condition, which has led their physician to forbid their impos-ing any strain upon it, should consult him or her before practising any of these exercises. This is because the latter do achieve their results by imposing strains.

Those whose advancing age suggests a similar carefulness may, with their physician's prior consent, take up the easiest only of these exercises. But they ought to proceed toward mastery very patiently and by very slow degrees.

141

I have seen an elderly Oriental successfully master some of these exercises at the age of sixty-three, and heard him speak of their beneficial results. Aged persons should approach such methods cautiously and slowly, but they need not let themselves be frightened away altogether merely because they are aged.

142

It should be understood that the seeker does not need to undertake all the exercises presented here. He should select those that seem best suited to him, or experiment where he is uncertain until he finds those which prove most useful.

143

The technique which suited those ancient conditions will not quite fit our modern ones. Those who disregard this fact open a door to mental derangement.

144

It would be certainly foolish to perform any of these exercises on a full stomach, and imprudent at least to perform them at a time or in a place where the temperature is excessively hot.

145

An isolated physical exercise is futile. Three minutes every day is better than one hour once a week.

146

Coordination: The way the mind takes hold of the body and muscles.

147

Exercises get reduced in value if done only occasionally. It is better, and in the end easier, if a regular habit is formed.

148

All these yoga exercises and physical practices are praiseworthy. They are recommended to aspirants—but only as accessories. They are not, and never can be, substitutes for that moment-to-moment struggle with the ego in daily living which is fundamental and inescapable. No forcible holding of the breath and no strained contortion of the body can take its place. The attempt to avoid following this discipline of the ego by substituting disciplines of the breath or flesh is a futile one, if it is an attempt to take the kingdom of heaven by violence. It cannot be successful. This desire to enter the kingdom in a hurry is pardonable. Yet if it were fulfilled the fulfilment would be a premature attainment and consequently lacking in fullness, falling short in wholeness, and uncertain of steadiness. All the different stages of development are needed in experience and can be missed only to our loss. Although timelessness is the quest's end, the journey itself must take place in the measured pace of time to prepare us properly for this end. It may be that this is because we may not take hold of spiritual possessions which we have not rightfully earned by personal labours and to which we have no honest legal title. It may be that a spiritual treasure cannot become our own in advance of the requisite efforts to develop adequate fitness and understanding for such vast responsibility.

6

BREATHING EXERCISES

The positive dynamic effects of deep breathing are well known. This is because with the indrawing breath, the deep inhalation, the mind is set positively and affirmatively; it is then taking advantage of the natural fact that the person's life-force is being drawn upon. If, however, we consider what happens when breath is exhaled, we see the process is reversed. During the interval between the exhalation and the next inhalation it is the universal life-force which then flows into the man because he is then passive, whereas when inhaling he was active. Now this universal life-force, when it expresses itself in man, acts as a link with the universal spirit and demands physical existence. In other words, when the breath is let out and briefly held before it is indrawn again, there is a bridge to the higher consciousness of man. The bridge is there, but he must take advantage of it and usually he does not. If, during those few moments of pause, he turned his mind into meditation upon his true being, he would find it easier then than at other times; or if he did the same thing after having had an unexpected glimpse, he could retain the uplift of the glimpse for a longer period.

2

The practice of breathing, when done as an exercise—whether sitting or walking—can be harmonized with a cosmic breath; that is, breathe out slowly, prolonging the outgoing breaths, so that the intake will come of itself naturally. While breathing out, mentally direct the air downwards towards the diaphragm. While breathing in, mentally connect with the cosmic life-force. Remember that the purpose of this lengthened out-breath is not only to empty the lungs of the stale air, but also to empty the mind of negative thoughts.

3

It will help to empty the mind of its tumult and the nerves of their agitation if he will breathe out as fully as possible, inhaling only when the first feeling of discomfort starts. He should then rest and breathe normally for several seconds. Next, he should breathe in as deeply as possible. The air is to be kept in the lungs until it is uncomfortable to do so. This alternation completes one cycle of breathing. It may be repeated a number of times, if necessary, but never for a longer period than ten minutes.(P)

4

The other breathing exercise which is dangerous—not physically so much as mentally—is that which prescribes breathing through alternate nostrils so that one nostril is closed by a finger and only the other is used until the changeover is made to the other nostril. This exercise is the one that threatens sanity. I would enforce as a rule that everyone who sets up to teach hatha yoga to others should be compelled to go through a course of at least one year in the anatomy of the body and then in the physiology of the body. The work must have a scientific basis because it encroaches on the medical domain.(P)

5

Revitalizing Breath Exercise: (1) Stand at an open window, spine erect, body straight, hands tightly holding hips. (2) Expel all stale air through the mouth. (3) Take three short, sharp sniffs of air and expel the total quantity in one long-drawn exhalation. Pause and breathe normally. Repeat three times. (4) Breathe in deeply through the nose, starting as low in the abdomen as possible, rising upward in the lungs until the upper part is filled. (5) The mind should concentrate on the solar plexus behind the navel. Imagine a stream of golden-white energy being drawn from there and radiated throughout the body. (6) Pucker up the lips and let all the air out as vigorously as possible. Tighten the diaphragm muscle while doing so, and move it upwards. Pause and breathe normally. Repeat three times.(P)

6

Breathing Exercise: A useful exercise which I have mentioned in one of the earlier books is to breathe out slowly and then let the inbreath come of itself, naturally. While breathing out, hold the thought of throwing out all negative thoughts and undesirable emotions. I ought to add now to the description of that exercise that this exhalation should last as long as possible without undue discomfort and that it should be originated in the region of the diaphragm—the abdomen or behind the navel. Keep the spine upright, with the head and neck in line with it. This enables you to better receive cosmic currents of life-force. It also strengthens the power of self-control, of disciplining the body.

7

The Death-Gasp Breathing Exercise: Lie flat on your back. Take a deep, quick inhalation through the open mouth, accompanied by the gasping half-loud shriek which such an act involuntarily produces. Then gradually and slowly exhale again.

This breathing exercise tries to imitate the death cry of dying creatures, the vocal expression of their fear of death. Such an imitation of the physical side of dying should bring with it, momentarily, the associated death fear whose gravity and importance naturally swallow up all lesser fears. If this exercise is done twice daily, these lesser fears gradually become weaker, while the fear of death is itself overcome.

8

If the hatha yogis are right, if the way to the kingdom of heaven is nasal and atmospheric, then why should we trouble to become unselfish, disciplined, and intelligent? Why bother to improve our characters at all? No! the wise student does not need breathing exercises although he may use them.

9

The power of the inheld breath to augment the body's energy is striking. A heavy weight which one could hardly lift ordinarily can be lifted much more easily if a deep, long breath is first taken and the air is retained in the lungs while attempting the feat. A long forward leap or a high jump can be more successfully achieved by following the same method.

10

Health and strength are to a limited extent in ratio to lung power. It is needful to practise deep breathing and take long breaths.

11

Breathing Exercise to Improve, Control, and Prevent Colds: Take in a series of six short breaths through the mouth very quickly, hold the air in the lungs for about two or three seconds, then let it out in a single, easy exhalation.

12

When deep breath is united to keen thought, and when the fused result is driven upwards physically to the brain and mentally in lofty aspiration to the Soul, the visitant will know by a beautiful change of consciousness that it is welcome.

13

Chuang Tzu also said that the pure men of old drew breath from their innermost depths, whereas the vulgar, only from their throats. We might say, this is equivalent to breathing from the point of the *hara*: a slow, deep breathing from behind the diaphragm.

14

The importance of diaphragmatic breathing is not only a physical one, because full breathing enables us to get the full manifestation of the life-force in the body, but also because it allows for a fuller and freer manifestation of the mind.

15

The danger of taking to these breathing exercises for the sake of developing personal powers is that if the powers are finally gained, the spiritual path is often lost.

16

Deep breathing practised in the shade of fir trees is not only invigorating, but beneficial to the lungs.

17

Breathing exercise to pacify mind and body: (1) lie flat on back with closed eyes; (2) breathe in fully, then hold breath for three seconds; (3) exhale, and restore normal breathing to get comfortable. This completes one cycle. Repeat it for a complete cycle of seven repetitions. Further instruction for use and development of this exercise must be obtained from a qualified teacher.

18

Those who wish to invigorate themselves quickly should practise for two or three minutes what has been variously called deep breathing, diaphragmatic breathing, and abdominal breathing. Expel the breath vigorously, then with palms resting on the lower ribs take in very slowly a deep breath, stretching out the diaphragm muscle while doing so, then exhale somewhat less slowly. Repeat this exercise until feeling freshly renewed. A variant of this is practised in hatha yoga, but it is not recommended to those working without a competent hatha yoga teacher, because it has its own dangers. This variant consists in holding the breath before exhaling it and the exhalation itself is done with a hissing noise. All breath holdings can be dangerous. If the breath is held for too long, consciousness is lost, and what is too long for one person may not be for another.

19

The practice of breath control (*pranayama*) may be viewed in terms of its goals, the means to attain them, and possible misuses of the practice.

Goals of breath control include: to reduce the number of wandering thoughts; to stop wandering thoughts completely; potential production of a glimpse; lengthening of a glimpse, if obtained; and bringing about a glimpse if lost.

The most common means of achieving these goals through breath practices are dual, and include the holding of the breath for short, safe periods, and the equalizing of the in and out breaths.

Dangers of breath control, if improperly practised, include: holding the breath for too long a period, causing a feeling of suffocation; the arisal of noticeable pressure on the heart; and a feeling that the lungs are about to burst. These warnings do not imply waiting to suspend practice until the problem occurs. It is more prudent to stop before the danger line is reached.

20

An aspirant came to Swami Ramdas and complained that, practising the instruction given him by a guru, he had done breathing exercises. These had ruined his health to the degree of forcing him to resign from a high government post. Ramdas often warned his disciples and visitors that these hatha yoga breath exercises were not meant for those living in the world, but for yogis who had withdrawn from it, and especially for those who were totally celibate.

21

Whether or not breathing exercises should be practised depends upon what feelings they arouse in the individual. If there are indications that they are leading to undesirable physical or psychical results, one should remember that progress can be made equally well without them if greater emphasis is placed on prayer.

22

Aspirational thought should not be suspended during breathing exercises, but should, on the contrary, be combined with them. Breath control is primarily intended to help still the mind, but it is not enough by itself to bring results.

23

The only safe breathing exercises to follow are given in the books. There are many other breathing exercises, but they are useless for the Western seeker and will positively NOT give him the higher consciousness he seeks. They will certainly produce queer effects, beautiful reveries, or refreshing deep sleep, but one can get the same results by using hashish or opium, and with less trouble. Neither Truth nor Peace can be got via the nose. There is only one way to arrive at the goal he seeks and that is by disciplining thought in meditation and concentration, and then using it for all it is worth in enquiry into the meaning of life.

24

There are great dangers in the indiscriminate practice of yoga breathing exercises. Even the one given in Vivekananda's books causes much havoc among Western students and in his later years Vivekananda himself greatly regretted having published it. Breath control is a sharp-edged instrument which can be very serviceable and yet at the same time very dangerous. A safe exercise which may be practised without a teacher is that given in Dr. Brunton's books. An abnormal nervous condition and ganglion trouble may well result from the ill-informed experiment of holding the breath.

25

The forceful retention of breath used in the yoga of body control was found by Buddha to be most painful as well as exciting to the nervous system, and it was only when he sat under the tree where he attained Nirvana that he found and practised the superior method which harmonized well with his lofty aim. An exercise which is largely identical with the one practised by the Buddha has been given in *The Secret Path* and *The Quest of the Overself*. The essence of it consists in breathing as gently and slowly as possible as is consistent with comfort for a few minutes prior to the actual practice of meditation. Thus the taking in and giving out of the breath is brought under temporary control. During the operation, attention should be wholly directed towards it, so that the student is fully conscious of the entire breath movement and of nothing else. This exercise is particularly recommended to remove thoughts of depression, bitterness, and unhappiness. Its chief aim, however, is to help bring down the upspringing thought waves to a calm surface and thus merge the numerous separate thoughts in undifferentiated Thought. Students of the ultimate path can just as usefully practise it as a preliminary to their mental exercise and it will be just as valuable to them. Two points ought, however, to be added to the description given in those books: the first being the necessity of keeping the torso erect so as to help and not hinder the respiratory process, and the second being that the breathing is not to be done by raising and lowering the shoulders but by raising and lowering the diaphragm so that the muscular region affected lies between the stomach and the chest.

26

The exercises in breath control are intended to affect the nervous system, or the psychic centres, or the bodily muscles, or certain organs according to which exercise is practised.

27

The first movement after waking up in the morning is intended to drive off drowsiness. It is practised by completely exhaling all stale air from the lungs and then deeply inhaling pure fresh air.

28

By watching the incoming and outgoing breath, its rhythm naturally slows down, thus calming the violent action of heart, lungs, and diaphragm. The heart pumps about seventeen tons of blood a day, and gets no rest at night, hence is the most overworked organ in the body. The ancients knew this method of resting the heart, thus increasing the span of life and also liberating a tremendous amount of life power, which revitalizes the cells of the body.

29

The highest achievement of the yoga of body control which is effected through certain breathing exercises is the state of utter unconsciousness of the physical body and of the physical world. Although this also effectively stops the process of generating thoughts, its result must not be confused with that stoppage which is attained in the intermediate or advanced mystic exercises. It is quite true to say that before or during the deep-trance state to which these breathing exercises eventually lead, the yogi's body can show remarkable powers; it may be buried under ground for hours or even days and emerge unharmed; it may be stabbed with knives but suffer hardly any loss of blood; its heart and lung action may cease entirely so far as finger and stethoscope tests may be able to ascertain; and corrosive poisonous acids may be poured into its stomach without hurting its membranous lining.

30

Chinese yoga: Breathe in very gently and hold the breath for the longest possible time. Breathe out just as gently. This gives mental abstraction.

31

The exercise requires him to empty the lungs thoroughly of all air, to wait two or three seconds, and to fill the lungs again slowly and deeply. At the same time, by using his creative imagination and his concentrated will, he commands the lower energy and consecrates it to lofty aspiration.

32

Transmutation exercise: Breathe in deeply and repeatedly. At the same time, definitely direct the energy to achieve magically and to create mentally whatever specific physical or mental objective is aspired to. It becomes a vehicle of sacred consecration, born from the transmutation of sex fluid into spiritual force. Thus a white magic ritual is performed, not for emotive relief but to start a new current of creative power. It may be done along with prayers and declarations.

33

If the retention of breath, which is the praised aim of hatha yogis, were enough by itself to confer spiritual benefits, then the pearl fishers who dive far below the surface of the waters of the Arabian Sea and Indian Ocean holding their breath for several minutes should feel and show these benefits too. But no report of such a result has ever been made.

34

Inhaling deeply is a health-giving exercise which revives spirits and cures depression. But this is so only provided the air is sent to the bottom of the lungs and thus expands the diaphragm. Expanding the lungs sideways is not enough. They must also be expanded in a downward direction.

35

Breathing exercises are best done in the morning. This is because the air is then purest, the body most in need of stimulation and awakening, the mind most ready to join with the breath in influencing the whole person.

36

A yogic breathing exercise which is really useful and danger-free combines constructive thinking with deep breathing. On the inhalation, the student is to imagine he is strengthening his will by transmuting his lower forces; on the exhalation he is to imagine that he is casting out emotional weakness and rubbish. The breaths should be deeper than usual, forceful "like a pair of bellows powerfully manipulated by a smith," as an ancient Hindu text says.

37

These breathing exercises are safe only if certain abstentions are practised. The chief of them are chastity, teetotalism, and non-smoking.

38

What does he seek to do by practising a process of breath control? First, the freeing of his mind from distractions and wanderings; second, the awakening of the "spirit-heat." The deeper the breathing, the greater the power awakened.

39

There is another reason besides Nature's stillness or environmental quietness for choosing dusk, dawn, or midnight, and that is the balanced breathing which temporarily follows. This in turn steadies the mind. At other times the breath passes more through the left or through the right nostril—disequilibrium which affects the mind.

40

The Hebrew Bible allots seventy years as the human life-span but the Hindu Vedic scripture which is far older, allots a hundred years. It is a curious fact that the ancient *Svarodaya Manual of Yoga* reported man as breathing three times less each minute than he generally does today. This means that each breath was longer in those early days when he lived out a century of years.

41

When the breath is deliberately inhaled or exhaled gently and evenly as an initial period of the meditation practice, the mind is slowly forced into a calm and concentrated mood.

42

The outgoing breath is not less important in its influence on the mind. If it is to contribute to the attainment of tranquillity, it should be so gentle that powder in a hand held to the nose would not be blown away. A forcible or violent exhalation obstructs the rising of the desired mental state.

43

Since the primary purpose of these exercises is to contribute toward the general attempt to gain control of the mind, to lessen and quieten the activity of thinking, to bring a settled calm into the entire consciousness, and to soothe and pacify the emotions, the primary means used is to establish a rhythm by breathing at a measured rate.

44

All breathing exercises should be done with the head, neck, and spine erect, hence done standing or sitting upright. This is partly because the spinal cord is ultimately affected by them, and should be kept free for the passage through it of nerve currents, and partly because the cerebellum at the nape of the neck is likewise ultimately affected by the passage of nerve currents through it.

45

Because I gave out an exercise (in *The Quest of the Overself*) in gentle, shallow breathing to be done for not more than five or six minutes when preparing for meditation in order to help induce the proper condition of calmness, some wrongly understood this to be a recommendation to be practised constantly throughout the day, and for a special purpose. To do it as a settled way of breathing was never advised and ought never to have been misread into the published instructions. On the contrary, for habitual day-long use I advise always and prescribe with conviction the method of deep diaphragmatic breathing as one to be adopted as customary.

46

Draw the Force into every pore of your skin until it pervades your whole body.

47

Breathing exercises should never be pushed to excess, for then they may become very dangerous. It is safer to underpractise them than to overdo them.

48

Why do people sigh agitatedly or catch their breath when hearing unexpected news about a relative's death? Is this not a sign that breath is the brother of thought?

49

The breath-watching exercise is a useful one. Keep the current of attention firmly fixed on the current of breath itself for a few minutes. Thus breathing becomes converted temporarily from an unconscious into a conscious process.

50

With every inhaled breath, draw in mentally also the calm strength, the renewal of poise which you need most at the time.

51

The combination of deep abdominal breathing with high spiritual aspiration forms an excellent exercise which is simple, easy, and effective. It gives a momentum to the positive and ennobling forces of the whole being.

52

The practice of equalizing the time periods of the incoming and outgoing breaths makes for a balanced flow of the nervous currents. This leads in turn to better control of the nerves and feelings. It is therefore a desirable exercise for those emotional types of persons who need it.

53

It is not only during set periods that he is to practise these slow, deep, and long breaths, but as frequently throughout the day as possible. In this way, it will become his habitual pattern of normal breathing.

54

The state of his breathing shows also the state of his feelings, his mind, and even his will.

55

Since the breath and the seed are man's most vital and valuable energies, they must be rightly used; they cannot be left out of such a scheme of purification and transformation.

56

A warning must be given that the regular occurrence of pain or of acute discomfort during the practice of any of these exercises ought to be taken as a red signal to abandon it. Otherwise an injury may result.

57

Clare Booth Luce, formerly an ambassador to Italy, once told how when she practised breathing exercises her body became cataleptic, as though dead, while she saw it lying inert from above. That stopped her exercising!

58

Deeper and fewer breaths will be needed by a vital, healthy man than by a weakly, sicker one.

59

The relaxed tension-free life brings with it a loss of nervousness, and this in turn a loss of the desire to smoke tobacco. The practice for a few minutes daily of slowing down breathing to half the usual rate is an exercise which affects blood circulation and slows it down, too. This indirectly helps to reduce the desire to smoke.

60

All breathing exercises should begin by cleansing the lungs with a thorough exhalation.

61

The man who is being treated in the Indian jungle for a snakebite, and whose wound must be cut out with a knife, is told to hold his breath during the cutting operation. Why?

62

In the Japanese art of karate, which can disable a man immediately by a blow with the side of the hand upon sensitive areas of the neck or throat, it should be noted that the art is performed on the *outgoing breath*.

63

The breathing exercises of yoga have results beyond the physical. They cleanse the emotional nature and purify the nervous system.

64

When the breathing is reduced to a few counts per minute, the production of poisonous carbon dioxide is reduced, too; the operation of the heart becomes calmer as the flow of blood slows down, the oxidation in the brain gets less, and the head feels markedly lighter. The rest of the body seems vaporous as if half-anesthetized. Thoughts are fewer and less insistent, the mind tending towards inactivity.

65

Inattention during this practice will produce sleep, whilst concentrated attention will bring a tingling sensation of Divine Life to every cell in the body. By faithful concentration we eventually learn to focus the mind and its power on any desired line of thought and hold it there, free of distinction. This enables us to rightfully seek a solution for every problem, and bit by bit opens up for us a greater and more fascinating spiritual horizon.

7

SEX AND GENDER

Philosophy approaches the subject of sex, marriage, love, and celibacy in a perfectly sane and rational way, but without the limitations and without the ignorance of a merely materialistic rationalism. Consequently, it grades the counsels which it gives on two levels.

It is not concerned with the average man who is not particularly interested in more than an average good life within the fold of conventional aims and needs.

The first level is for the beginning quester who has set his aims and needs somewhat higher than the average man and who is willing to undergo a moderate discipline for this purpose.

The second is for the more advanced quester who seeks to attain the highest possible standard and who is willing to pay in self-denial and self-training the corresponding price.

The beginner's counsel allows him a disciplined sex life, with the extent of the discipline being set by himself, for no general rule which would cover the widely varying circumstances, responsibilities, obligations, and characters involved can possibly fit them all. It explains the nature of the sex force and then leaves it to him to decide how far and how fast he wishes to go with its control.

The second grade counsel is almost monastic in its disciplinary demand for it bids him refrain from the sex relation altogether, save for the purpose of having children, whose number must be limited and proportioned strictly. In the case of the unmarried, there will then be a complete chastity.

No counsel can be given to the attained philosopher, for since he is able to reabsorb the sex urge successfully, completely, spontaneously, and unconsciously there is no urge, desire, or passion felt in this direction at all. Consequently, there is no need here for any kind of discipline. Nevertheless if, being married, he should decide to have children there is equally nothing to stop him from entering into the sexual act for this purpose. When that happens it will not be at the bidding of any lower urge, but out of willingness to provide a physical vehicle for the high-grade ego or egos he, and his wife, expect to attract.

2

That Nature put the hunger instinct into man and animal alike primarily to preserve the life of the physical body and not to satisfy the palate, nobody could rightly deny. The enjoyment of food is subordinate to, and intended to make more inescapable, the instinct required for this highly important necessity of sustenance. Yet man, blinded by his desires and passions, fails to see that the same situation prevails to explain part (not all) of the sexual instinct. Nature is not interested in his individual pleasure so much as in the continuance of his species. She has given him the one for the sake of the latter. Man has in thought, belief, and practice today reversed this order of importance. The result is a totally wrong view about the possibility and value of continence. From this view stems a host of moral, nervous, and physical maladies which are plunging his life into confusion and disaster. Diderot, the French thinker and encyclopaedist of the eighteenth century, in his anti-religious writing drew attention to the harm caused by emotional repression to nuns; what he particularly had in mind was sexual repression. The mystic has sometimes used erotic images when describing his experience. In the case of nuns this has been interpreted by modern sceptics, and especially by psychoanalysts, to indicate frustrated sexual desire. Such a condition must have been true of some nuns but cannot possibly have been true of the more advanced ones. For a certain part of the mystic experience during deep meditation does correspond in several details to the sexual experience. There is, in these moments, a surrender of the attitude of being in control of oneself, a conscious recognition and acceptance of another entity which is allowed to take possession and work on oneself. In consummated sexual love, the feeling of union is an intense one, but it is a union of two unlike entities. In realized mystical experience, the longing for union between the ego and what is beyond it is equally intense, and there is likewise here a marriage of two unlike entities—the passive willing ego giving itself up in ecstasy to the mysterious and impersonal higher power.

Nature has her rights, it is true, but before we can justly grant them we need to inquire as to what they really are. Her instincts in us are often perverted.

We have to enquire why it is that most religions severely judged and deprecated the sexual instinct, and why they recommended its subjugation to their elite of priests and monks. It is the strongest of bodily instincts, the supreme expression of physical life, and therefore the possible gateway to a complete surrender to materialism. Materialism achieves its greatest triumph in the inflamed and total self-identification of man and woman with their material bodies. In this absolute ecstasy of interlocked flesh there is no thought or place for the spirit, no care for memory of its existence. The infatuated man, who finds his beloved immeasurably desirable, will be restless or even tormented until he can achieve union with her. Absolute asceticism and rigid monasticism were set up as preventives against such a surrender. Only by sheer flight from temptation, it was believed, could there be any possibility of successful subjugation.

Gandhi demonstrated in his own person the foolishness of the belief that absolute continence leads to mental disorder. He was sane enough to lead his countrymen to freedom. He also demonstrated the falsity of the belief that it was impossible. For forty years he practised it successfully. He said: "The ability properly to conserve, assimilate, and transmute the vital fluid comes with long training. It strengthens the body and the mind." His spiritual career further indicated that mastery of sex by those who have experienced it is more likely to be real and lasting than in the case of those who have starved it.

3

In India the traditional view has allotted women a role inferior to that of men. It is generally held that fewer women than men have ever attained the higher goals. Indeed, in some of the sacred works which have come down from ancient times and which still govern much of the thinking upon the subject today, the spiritual aspirant who has obtained a male birth is regarded as being much more fortunate than one who has obtained a female one.

One of the major reasons why women have been assigned a lower status for so long a time has been, aside from the selfish social exploitation of her physical weakness, the asceticism which belongs to the mystical stage of development. Such asceticism has often taken an extreme and unbalanced form with the result that the values and virtues of monastic celibacy have been overrated and the dangers symbolized by women have been exaggerated. On the philosophic level the balance is restored, extreme fanatic views are dispelled, and the natural relationship between the sexes seen in its true light. Philosophy has no use for mere asceticism although it has plenty of use for self-discipline. According to this teaching there are three states of spiritual development: first, religious; second, mystical or metaphysical; third, philosophical. In the first stage, women are overwhelmingly ahead of men. In the second stage, women and men are roughly equal in the success of their attainment. In the third and final stage, it is mostly men who succeed. A brief explanation why this is so appears in Chapter 5 of *The Hidden Teaching Beyond Yoga* [see last paragraph before "Give up the Ego!" —Ed.].

This said, all souls are of equal importance before God. The soul, in the sense of the true self, has no sex whatever. Personalities, which are its projections, may vary their sex from birth to birth, if we accept the theory of reincarnation, and therefore the important thing is not the sex to which we belong, but the inner mental being that we are. Of great importance are the evolutionary changes through which mankind in general has been passing during recent centuries. Women have been exploited and subjected by men for ages past and it is only within recent times that they have begun to come into their own and claim the rights and privileges which are their just due. In the coming age, balance will be restored and woman will take her rightful place alongside of man in the leadership of the whole race.

To sum up, it is no longer a question of what the ancients believed about women or how the modern Indians regard them, but a question of accepting the evolutionary trend of things which is bringing the human race closer and closer to enlightenment and thus making it possible for every woman to claim and receive what is best in life if she wishes.

4

These animal desires belong to the body. What are we? Are we that or a mind using a body? Or Mind using a mind and a body? This last is indeed the truth. When we find it out for ourselves, and hold to it through the years, how long can these desires keep their strength? We may be assured that they dwindle and go.

5

This divineness of its origin disproves the slurs cast on sex by those ascetics who wrongly regard it as an evil. It is the lack of proper control and knowledge or the abuse and misdirection of sex that turn it into an evil; but until man slowly evolves into awareness of his true self, it will continue to provide him—along with Art and Nature—with feelings of happiness which relieve the gloom of earthly life. Yet, in contrast to the happiness gained from Art and Nature, and much more to that gained from spiritual awareness, there are heavy penalties for the abuse, misdirection, or lack of control of sex force.

6

In the creative sublimation of the passions—especially lust and wrath—lies the source of impressive spiritual energy leading to satisfying achievement. Only by personal experience can it be rightly judged how valuable is the practice of storing up the innermost essence of sexual force by creative and informed abstinence, and then transforming this force into positive qualities, and how greatly it develops the power of will. This does not necessarily mean a surrender to absolute asceticism, although that is perfectly possible and beneficial if carried out in the right spirit, but it does mean periods of relative asceticism.

7

This co-operation of mind, will, and breath to redirect the sexual energy is its true transformation into a non-sexual kind. This is completely different from, and superior to, the alleged sublimation into art, work, or intellect proffered by psychoanalysts, or into sport and physical exercise proffered by educators. These may reduce the strength of sex urges, or diminish their frequency, or cause them to vanish altogether, but such a result will hold for a time only and will not be a lasting one. For it is attained by a process which temporarily exhausts the urge but does not confront and conquer it at all. A peasant who is too tired after a very heavy day's toil to attempt intercourse has not sublimated his sex energy in any way and may even indulge in imaginary acts of intercourse while he lies physically fatigued. The case of the sports enthusiast or gymnast is not too dissimilar from the peasant's. Nor is the case of the intellectual or artist, although on an entirely different plane, really different in principle. When the intellectual work or artistic activity comes to an end, what is to stop the man's mind working in a sexual direction if his tendencies are strongly that way?

The philosophic method of sublimation comes to the problem by looking sex in the face, understanding its place and purpose, and dealing with it on mental and psychic as well as physical levels. The aim here is not mere repression, not deceptive pseudo-sublimation, but full mastery.

8

The man who struggles with the passion of sex within his nature and conquers it, not merely physically but also mentally, finds that his very nature becomes bi-sexual. For he finds within himself the woman whom he had formerly sought outside himself. She who was to complement his mind and companion his body, and whom he could only find in an imperfect form or not find at all, is then discovered within his own spirit, in that which is deeper than body and mind. The mysterious duality which thus develops corresponds to the last stage but one of his mystical progress, for in the last stage there is absolute unity, absolute identity between his own ego and his Overself; but in the penultimate stage there is a loving communion between the two, and hence, a duality. Such a man is in need of no fleshly woman, and if he does marry it will be for reasons other than the merely conventional ones. In achieving this wonderful liberation from the drawbacks which accompany the delights of sex and from the shortcomings which modify its promises, he achieves something else; he enters into love in its purest, noblest, most divine, and most exalted state. Thus his nature is not starved of love as shallow observers may think or as the sensual-minded may believe, but only he, rather than the others, knows what it means. Seemingly he stands alone, but actually he does not. He is conscious of a loving presence ever in him and around him, but it is love which has shed all turmoils and troubles, all excitements and illusions, all shortcomings and imperfections.

It is hard to overcome sexual desire, and neither ashamed repression nor unashamed expression will suffice to do so. Hunger and surfeit are both unsatisfactory states. The middle way is better, but it is not a solution in the true meaning of this term.(P)

9

At the time when a child is conceived, two factors contribute powerfully towards its physical nature and physical history. They are the state of the father's thinking and the mother's breathing.(P)

10

The sex urge, bodily urge, physical attraction, animal urge—is often covered with romantic or sentimental tinsel and called love.

11

That most human beings make their paradise depend on the mere friction of paired bodies is something for a planetary visitor to marvel at.

12

Overpopulation has increased the poverty of the underdeveloped world. Overpopulation is due to oversexed activity. The belief that sex is here solely for pleasure is universal. The belief that it is here solely to produce wanted children with sex thrown in as an inducement is usually rejected. But the second belief is the correct one. Man has abused his sex instinct so that only its exaggerated continued act is considered normal and proper!

13

The standpoint from which the question of sex is best approached was explained in my book, *The Wisdom of the Overself*. It is neither pro-ascetic nor anti-ascetic. The man who is called to the spiritual quest is also called to engage in a battle with his animal instincts. If they are to rule him, he will never know peace. And sex being one of the most powerful of such instincts, it must necessarily be brought under control and disciplined. This is true of all its three phases: mental, emotional, and physical. It is quite possible, healthy, and natural for a man to live a perfectly continent life for many years, the sperm being re-absorbed into the body, provided his mental life is kept equally pure. This is achieved by constant reflection upon the matter from the standpoints of experience, observation, and idealism, as well as by deliberate sublimation when passion is felt. Those who say the sperm must be got rid of are merely making intellectual concessions to their own moral weakness. But on the other hand, it is equally true that if a man does not feel able to rise to such a standard, he may live a normal married life and yet make spiritual advancement provided he disciplines himself firmly, keeps constantly in view the limited nature of sex satisfactions, nurtures the incessant yearning for and love of the Soul, and especially seeks to purify his thought-life. There are different requirements about the extent and nature of sex discipline at different stages of the path. Your own innermost promptings are the best guide here for they come from the higher self. But they need to be separated from bodily impulses and emotional broodings, which is difficult to do. It is immaterial for the adept whether he lives a celibate or married life. The attitude toward sex will always depend upon individual circumstances.

14

A celibacy reached through insight and not by institutional behest, or an asceticism practised within marriage—in both cases as immaculate in thought as in deed—shows its value in peace and strength. But for those who cannot arrive at this admittedly difficult condition, there should be periods of temporary withdrawal from sex activity ranging from a few weeks to a few years. For single persons and dedicated married ones it is a voluntary inner self-discipline.

15

Under the urge of sexual passion men will form undesirable relationships which bring mental and emotional sufferings, or fall into unpleasant habits, or behave quite ridiculously under the delusion that they are finding happiness.

16

To gratify the desire of the moment without thought about its possible distant, but undesirable, consequence, is the act of a child. If a man wishes to become truly adult he should cultivate the needful qualities.

17

The price of excess pleasure has to be paid in the end. It is paid in unwanted children, unhappy castaways, unpleasant diseases, lost health, and premature ageing.

18

Strength is squandered in undisciplined sexual activity.

19

If he is to lift himself above the improper beguilements of sex, this is not to say that he is to lift himself above the proper functions of sex.

20

The passage from D.H. Lawrence to Brother Lawrence is the passage from a mysticism that exaggerates sexual desire to a mysticism that ignores it. Either attitude is ill-balanced. A philosophical mysticism must revolt against both Lawrences, for it cannot risk the madness which shadows the modern one, nor be satisfied with the incompleteness of the medieval one.

21

When the mating urge descends on men or women, they develop a temporary but immense capacity for glorifying the beloved person, seeing beauties and virtues which may be quite slight or even non-existent. With the eyes so widely out of focus, nature achieves her purpose with ease.

22

So long as the animal, with all its passions unruled, reigns over the man, so long as the body holds him captive, he will lack the strength to turn the mind far away from it and to concentrate his attention deep enough to get his release. The animal is honourable; it has no higher duty than to be itself, its natural self. So far as man has a body too, he shares this same search for repeated but fleeting physical and pleasurable sensations. But he alone has the faculty of higher abstract and metaphysical thought, with the sensitivity to feel intuitively the presence of a divine soul. Their development is his duty too.

23

In their inordinate desire to follow their own desires and to claim freedom from parents and other authority, too many among the young give themselves up to sexual intercourse, whether promiscuous or not, whether they use contraceptives or not, to an inordinate degree. In the end they become too irresponsible. When they marry the relationship is more likely to fall apart, the children to feel insecure and to become problem cases.

24

Unfulfilled sex tends to stir up new problems or affect old ones.

25

It is a stiff and saddening problem, this of the many people to whom a right opportunity for marriage has not presented itself. Yet it is saddening only so long as they fail to understand and master the sex forces involved; so soon as this poise is established and balance found within the self, there will be peace too.

26

The philosopher can find wisdom only in total abstinence because that best suits his own character. The man who has built a balanced nature finds such temperance a saner and safer path.

27

Just as Nature has hidden the mind's deepest secret and sublimest satisfaction in the centre of its being, so has she hidden woman's most mysterious function and joyous activity in the centre of her body.

28

The overwhelming emotion of romantic love subsides with time and then only does reason get a chance to be heard.

PBPF / Larson Publications
4936 State Route 414
Burdett, NY 14818-9729   USA

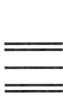

LARSON PUBLICATIONS

For regular updates on our new publications, please fill in your name and address (and/or those of interested friends or book dealers) and drop this card in the mail.

BOOK IN WHICH CARD WAS FOUND

_____

NAME

ADDRESS

NAME

ADDRESS

☐ Please send brochure on *The Notebooks of Paul Brunton* series.

29

Sex is an ancient primitive impulse. But today science has put at its disposal certain devices for its satisfaction without some of its undesired consequences.

30

The Freudian tenet that sex force is convertible into artistic creativeness arises out of a misunderstanding. The energy saved from disciplined sex strengthens the rest of the human personality, physically and mentally, but does not automatically turn itself into artistic power.

31

If the mere repression of sex impulses could turn an ordinary man into a genius, why have so many ascetics been intellectually or inventively sterile?

32

There are those among both sceptics and believers who equate the mystical experience of bliss with the sexual orgasm, but it is a poor equation.

33

There are troublesome opposing forces which will resist if you fight them, but serve if you use and redirect them with enlightenment. To some extent sex is one of these forces.

34

The reckless entry into marriage under the influence of physical passion is a sign of juvenility, of surrender to adolescent urges, whether the person is eighteen years old or fifty. He has not the patience to wait for a fuller mating nor the prudence to investigate to what he is really committing himself.

35

So-called romances do not necessarily concern love in its basic meaning, for possessiveness and jealousy may accompany them, or they may really belong to animal physiological attraction.

36

Most women who aspire to the Divine look for, and find comfort with, the idea or the image of a Personal God. For them the path of devotional love is more attractive than any other path. The strength of their emotional nature accounts for this. But male aspirants are generally more willing to take to the various non-devotional approaches. Their intellectual nature and their power of will are often stronger than those of women. It is easier for them to comprehend, and also to accept, the idea of an Impersonal God. For these, and for other reasons, although there have been many successful female mystics in history, there have been few successful female philosophers.

37

While the animal nature is the ruler, aided by human cunning or shrewdness, do not expect loftier aspiration to be forthcoming.

38

A man who has reconciled himself properly to the celibate state finds a freedom, a peace, which is his compensation.

39

Is it possible that out of a bodily embrace between two creatures this remarkable entity can be born—the human mind with all its qualities and attributes and spiritual possibilities?

40

Sexual union not only is something operative on the physical plane, but also on the psychic plane. This psychical union may be harmful to the higher-bred person of the two who are engaged in the intercourse.

41

The forty-eight or in some editions sixty-four postures described in the Hindu book on sex love called *Kama Sutra*, now widely translated and published in the West, are simply forty-eight or sixty-four ways for a man to lower himself to purely animal status. In fact several of them are given animal names by the author.

42

As villages, cities, countries, and whole civilizations grow in size their problems grow with it. The more people, the more problems. Today a fuss is being made about the dangers of the population explosion. But the only kind of remedy which the world considers seriously is mechanical or chemical birth control, the use of some kind of contraceptive. It does not seem to occur to most people that the root of the matter lies in their enslavement to sexual passions and that only a voluntary sex control arrived at by their own inner growth can deal with this problem without creating adverse or harmful side effects—whether personal or social—as the contraceptives are causing.

43

The desire to avoid the sufferings of pregnancy and childbirth may become so strong in a woman that in a further rebirth the sex may be channeled into desire for the safety of intercourse with a person of the same sex.

44

A woman should set out deliberately to cultivate those qualities tradi- tionally considered masculine and which men have acquired partly through a different physical organization and partly through conflict with the world and conduct of its affairs. That these qualities are latent in her is shown by the numerous cases of career women who have successfully established themselves in fields of action uninvaded before the nineteenth century. For instance, positive self-reliant character and rational practical judgement traditionally belong to man while a gentle character and emotion-swayed faith are traditionally feminine. She has acquired the latter for reasons of her own physical constitution and by caring for the family and tending its home. Man must set out to cultivate these two characteristics also and yet take care not to lose his more reasonable and logical way of thought while doing so, since this is needed to correct them. Both sexes must learn to let the impersonal intuition and impartial conscience control all the other functions and keep them in equilibrium. Neither sex is to lose those outward qualities which mark and distinguish the sexes from one another and render them attractive to each other. He is to remain manly, she to retain her femininity. The change will show itself mostly in reaction to others and in response to the world.

45

It is difficult for most women to carry out all the obligations of marriage and motherhood, and, at the same time, find the leisure and freedom for spiritual studies. Nevertheless, quite a number find it possible to do so. If real effort is made, and if it is accompanied by earnest prayer for Divine assistance, the higher self will see that the way gradually becomes easier.

46

It is true that many inhabitants of monasteries and convents allow the fear of sex to become dominant. But this is certainly not true of the philosophic mystic. The latter knows that unless an individual feels strongly impelled to discontinue physical relations, sexual abstinence may do considerably more harm—mentally and physically—than spiritual good. Therefore, the general attitude toward sex should be one of acceptance—but certain disciplines and ethical standards must, naturally, accompany it.

47

It is not necessary to try to kill out all sex desire before one can experience spiritual rebirth, but it is necessary to discipline it. Marriage is permissible, but the animal nature must be controlled by the higher Will.

48

Sometimes one asks whether it is right to indulge in sexual promiscuity because of urgent desires and thus to get the thing out of his system, as it were. The answer is given in *The Voice of the Silence*, which says: "Do not believe that lust can ever be killed out if gratified or satiated, for this is an abomination inspired by Satan. It is by feeding vice that it expands and waxes strong, like to the worm that fattens on the blossom's heart." Such methods of gratification never get it out of anyone's system. There are more effective and safer ways.

Meanwhile, meditation may help by mentally retracing premarital or even extramarital experiences of sex, but to see them this time from the ugly and repulsive side, with all the sordid little details and low principles, the risks and confusions, the futility and disappointment that mark the end, and thus get the other side of the picture. This kind of meditation is to be analytic and reflective. It is intended to create certain associative thoughts which will immediately manifest themselves whenever the desire itself manifests. Some attach too much importance to physical asceticism such as fasting and not enough to following out the evil consequences of sex desire by repeated thoughts and imaginations, until they are etched into his outlook.

49

Sexual promiscuity is dangerous for many reasons. This is so because: (1) The aspirant's karma becomes entangled with the other person's. (2) One becomes psychically infected with low thought-forms hovering in the other person's aura. (3) Philosophy requires its adherents to consider the effects of their actions upon the lives and the character of others. We are to help their evolution, not their retrogression. (4) Intercourse with many unevolved types gives a special shock to the nervous systems of those who practise meditation and disintegrates something of their achievements each time.

50

It is quite correct that there was a separation of the sexes in the far past but that was for evolutionary purposes, and belonged only to the lower levels of existence. Hence Jesus rightly explained that in heaven—the higher level of existence—there is neither marrying nor giving in marriage.

51

You have the good fortune or misfortune to be attractive to men and so long as you remain unmarried you may expect that they will importune you. It is of course a matter for you to decide how you are to react in every case; but to whether it is necessary to yield in order to get on in practical life, I would reply that many women do yield and do get on in consequence but it is not necessarily the only way to get on. It is the easier but a slippery and dangerous path and I would certainly advise you to try the harder way even though you may not get on so well in consequence. Every rose on the easier path has a thorn concealed beneath it. It is not that sex in itself is a sin, for at a certain evolutionary level it is a natural function, but that self-respect demands it should be an expression of something finer than mere barter. It is more satisfactory in the end to establish yourself materially through determination and courage than to yield to temptation. Another point is that promiscuous sex not infrequently leads to disagreeable entanglements of karma which have to be disentangled at the price of suffering. That is one of the several reasons why marriage has been laid down as the normal path for humanity.

52

From a certain time onwards, greater asceticism may be necessary. Dietary changes, with which the individual may experiment, are one step in the right direction. He should strive to improve his whole general condition. All matters involving self-restraint where diet, drinking, smoking, and so on, are concerned should be watched and inner promptings carefully followed. It is also advisable to have regular periods of complete chastity—partly to exercise and develop the will and partly to prepare oneself for the practice of higher meditation. Although a philosophic discipline rejects permanent and exaggerated forms of asceticism, it both accepts and uses occasional and intelligent ones.

53

It remains merely an animal act, an expression of the body's lust, and nothing more. The reasons are obvious and have prompted many spiritual aspirants, both Asiatic and Christian, to become celibates and monks. These reasons may not be so obvious to those who are obsessed by sex, as so many modern writers have been who have influenced the younger generations, who are stupefied by the sense-pleasure of it, who are slaves to its recurring habit-forming urges and understand nothing of the need for its discipline. The philosophers have long known that there is a higher view of sex, and some among them know that there is even a higher practice of it which eliminates the spiritual obstacle and raises it to the level of spiritual co-operation. This is brought about by substituting stillness for passion. Such a change cannot be achieved without the practice of physical, nervous, emotional, and mental self-control. Just as the high point of meditation provides its glorious result under the condition of a thought-free stillness, in the same way raising sex to this immeasurably higher octave requires the condition of an inward and outward immobilization. That this can be reached, that the coupling of the two sexes could possibly have any relationship with the higher development of man, may seem incredible to those who know only its passional side.

54

That inferior tantrik sects have eagerly used the teaching to make their sexual desires appear as holy aspirations is quite true. This is part of the danger in such methods and why they are held in ill repute by many Indian authorities.

55

The dragon of sex must be fought. It may be conquered, but its strength differs at different stages of the fighter's life.

56

Krishnamurti: "Chastity is a mind that is completely free from all image making, all the pictures, sensations, which thought has built in its search for pleasure through sex. Then you will find an abundance of energy."

57

Man and woman, having the power between them to create another human being, may use this power either in submission to animal urges or in consonance with their highest ideals. In the former case, only physical or social penalties will keep them from being unrestrainedly self-indulgent. In the latter case, only the serious decision by both parties to provide a bodily vehicle for a higher type of reincarnating ego will bring them together in the procreative act. Children will then owe their birth to the serious act and deliberate purpose of two calm, mature persons, not to the chance union and ungoverned passion of two drifting ones.

58

A substance so valuable that it can create another human being, must be used in accordance with its value, not squandered in unthinking indulgence.

59

History gives enough evidence to show that too many stern attempts to impose celibate ways of living unloosed some of the lusts they seek to bind. They could not be enforced on the unready.

60

If sexuality is an attribute of animal and human life, sexual love is an ordinary fact of human nature. Why should it be regarded as suspect, why should it be treated as anti-spiritual? If the answer is that the passions of sex drag man down into the mud, philosophy shows how they can be sublimated so as to lift him up to heaven. They can be brought to dismiss their ancient enmity towards spiritual aspiration, to unite and work together for man's redemption, his enlightenment, and his salvation.

61

Tolstoy took long cross-country walks and bicycle rides in the early period when he tried to eradicate all sex desires. Those who have no desire to go to the extreme length to which his highly ascetic turn took him, may nevertheless find cycling a helpful and healthy exercise.

62

When this process of balancing the two forces comes to an end, the male-female consciousness of the real human being will be established at last.

63

There is a hidden teaching on sex in the Orient. This is known as tantrik yoga. The full teaching has usually been unavailable to the general public because of the dangers of misunderstanding and misuse should it fall into the hands of the unready or unworthy. The other systems of yoga generally favour an ascetic and stoical attitude toward sex whereas the tantrik system does not. In this modern age when so much of the hidden teaching has been revealed so widely, there is no reason why the tantrik teaching should remain completely hidden. If properly placed in the setting of a system of self-discipline and self-development, and if properly expounded with reasons, causes, and effects made quite clear, if kept free from all the entangling symbolism which has grown around the teaching during the centuries, it may have something useful to contribute to modern knowledge and modern living.

64

The physical methods used by the early Christian desert ascetics to crush sex were not bad, although incomplete in themselves, and have been tested by time since then. They included fasting, abstinence from alcohol and meat and cooked food, sleeping on the floor, and running until exhausted.

65

The biological need of sex which is satisfied by marriage, must be respected even by the man who has renounced it. He ought not fall into the error of one kind of ascetic who denounces it in vituperative language or of the other kind who tries to ignore it in repressive silence. It is a perfectly natural function which becomes evil if man degrades it, noble if he elevates it, changed if he sublimates it.

66

The sex craving expires in giving birth to its transformation—the spirit-fire energy.

67

Where excessive erotic thinking accompanies physical continence, the result may be mental disorder or bodily sickness.

68

The children who would be born to parents whose matings are few, whose minds are pure, and whose hearts are aspiring, would be markedly superior in every way.

69

An enforced chastity, which is the product of rigid circumstances or lack of temptation, is not the philosophic chastity.

70

In these matters of sex, alcohol, and smoking we simply place the inner psychic and spiritual facts about them before the aspirant and and tell him that it is essential for the use of them to be a disciplined one. How far he should discipline them is entirely a matter for his personal decision. He may go only 5% or he may go all the way into 100% total abstinence, or all the range of points between.

71

The power of sex to make or mar happiness or equanimity is formidable. Left to run amok in savage lust it harms and degrades a man but, redeemed and transmuted, it serves his best interests.

72

He knows, by theory and practice, logic and experience, that chastity may conserve energy—physical and mental, emotional and spiritual. But he knows also that it creates undesired and undesirable effects in mind and character.

73

Chastity is not the same as purity, although the two are often confused. The one is a way of outward life; the other a state of inner life.

74

Such chastity cannot be avoided if the energies needed for mastering the mind are to become powerful enough. In most men sex is the largest diversion of these energies.

75

The true union between man and woman is tantrik. But it cannot be brought about without developed qualities on both sides.

76

Sex, which ought to be a natural controlled urge, has all-too-often become a disease, a fever, an obsession.

77

Those physical and passional conditions which pass for love among the young—with their uncontrollable sensuality, their total unconcern with higher values, their puppet-like copulation—all show that they have still to outgrow the close ties which they still have to the animal stage of evolution.

78

The idea of sexual pleasure is derived from, based upon, the pair of opposites—masculine, feminine. Like all other ideas it has to be transcended; like all other pairs of opposites, it has to be brought into equilibrium.

79

In the wild, ungoverned, unhealthy, and irresponsible atmosphere of sexuality which covers the younger generation's world today, we may find some explanation why it was regarded with suspicion, or opposed altogether, not so long ago.

80

They turn away from the passionate desires of the flesh; they seek an existence devoid of its animality. But, lacking esoteric knowledge, without understanding how spirit and body are interwoven, too often they suffer defeat.

81

So far as psychoanalysis confirms the demands of sexual craving without putting upon it the basic disciplines which health, character, and self-respect require, so far does it cease to be a therapy, and become an injury.

82

The enchantment and glamour in which lovers find themselves are too often false and deceptive, mere preliminary devices used by Nature to get them together and thus fulfil her larger purposes. The ancient Greek or Roman thinker who likened their condition to a form of madness was not so far wrong as he seems. But too often also it is subject to change; the glamour goes or is transferred elsewhere or, worse, is transformed into repulsion. And where sex is not the hidden operative factor, one of the two is a victim of—or possessed by—some other force: ambition, economic need, vanity, the power complex.

83

Sex polarity provides the force bringing the bodies of men and women into intermittent attractive relation, but mental polarity provides a more lasting one.

84

The strict discipline to which sex desire was subject in the earlier stages is abandoned in the later ones, for all lusts and wraths fall away of their own accord as his own growth, with the touch of grace, sets him free.

85

As the sex energy is transmuted by will and mentally distributed throughout every part of the body, it bestows physical strength and resistance to disease.

86

Where fate forces the practice of complete abstinence it should be accepted philosophically and its compensatory benefits recognized.

87

Lust rises like a fever, rages along its course, and then subsides. But between start and finish much of a lifetime may pass away.

88

When adolescent boys and girls are able to rush from one pleasure to another, from one emotional entanglement to another, without a thought of the consequences involved or of other persons concerned, except what contribution they can make to selfish enjoyment, when all this is done in the name of modern self-expression, then a state of moral danger can be said to exist. The Buddha suggested a philosophical way of controlling the animal passions in man. He affirmed that if we will think often of the inevitability of our own death, if we will remember that the upshot of all our activities is the funeral-pyre, the burial grave, we will begin to realize how pitiful, how ultimately worthless, and how immediately transient are all our passions. How will the animal passions appeal to the man lying on his deathbed? The thought of death even to those who are still very much alive will thus diminish the strength of lust, greed, hate, and anger.

89

The force which men spend in ungoverned sexual desire keeps them imprisoned in their lower nature. This same force can be sublimated by will, imagination, aspiration, prayer, and meditation. When this is done, the Overself can then instruct them for they will be able to hear its voice.

90

Few are willing to surrender sex; yet, because it is such a tyrant, it must be conquered *completely* if the Overself is to rule.

91

When this bipolar nature of sex is understood, when it is seen that the opposite pole is always contained in every being, the question arises whether marriage is needed any longer to achieve the balance of these two poles. The answer must be that so long as the need is *felt*, so long is the sex force still not sublimated and the development of the other pole within oneself still incomplete. Marriage will continue to be indicated until this completion is attained.

92

When men are asked to deny totally and permanently their sex instinct, they are asked too much. The force of human nature would overtake them in the end. An ideal which is unrealizable is useless as a working ideal, however lofty it seems as a theoretical one.

93

If the seed is expended then nerve energy is lost, the mind is debilitated and its power of upward contemplative flight reduced. But this does not necessarily lead to the consequence of a prohibition against marriage or to a refusal of its consummation. It leads to a discipline of marriage and to a change in its consummation. If philosophy rejects the ascetic view in this matter, it also rejects the common view and the common practice. More cannot be written in public print but let it suffice that both the finest relationship between the sexes and the highest purity in sexual ethics are attained only among the philosophical adepts. Theirs is not only a moral achievement but a magical one. The retention of semen is a practice in such circles as also in Indian yoga and Chinese Taoism.

94

The act of reproducing the human body can be made a sacred one or left an animal one. The monastic celibates are not the only persons who live what they call a "pure" life. Any married couple can do the same, provided they limit their physical relations to reproductive purposes alone and even then limit the number of their children to what reason and intuition direct.

This means that they will refuse to dissipate the generative energies for mere pleasure, but instead will deliberately seek to transmute them. Thus marriage is redeemed by the few who can rise to this lofty ideal, as it is degraded by the many who insist on keeping to their kinship with the animals.

95

If the seminal secretions of the sexual glands are conserved and if the sexual desires are mentally sublimated, the man will become self-possessed in speech and action. He will experience a joyous feeling of mastery over the animal in him that weaklings never know and cannot understand.

96

The soul-mate is really the Self within. He will find his true soul-mate when he finds his inner Self, when he yields himself completely and lovingly up to it.

97

The sexual need is an expression, in its grosser passion-swept form, of the unconscious belief in the reality of the physically sensed world. But in its subtler form it is an expression of belief in the reality of the ego. This becomes evident, however, only when a man transcends the ego in actuality, for then the need wholly falls away because the impulse behind it falls away.

98

I do not mean by chastity the mere compulsory celibacy of unmarried persons, for this can still be accompanied by—and often is—mental erotic indulgence or emotional erotic craving. I mean a state physically free from need of passion and emotionally secure from disturbance of fantasy.

99

Few escape being assailed by sex urges. Most rule them physically alone, and then only so far as a limited morality, prudence, or position requires. Few seek *mental* victory over them or even want such a victory. Since the battle is usually hard and long, these attitudes are understandable. But the Quester has no other option than to fight for self-mastery here as in other passional spheres.

100

The passion for the particular muscular or acrobatic exercise which is for most men their attraction to the opposite sex, is their inheritance from the animal evolution to which their bodies belong. It may of course be accompanied by higher attractions, admirations, or affections, or even covered up and masked by them.

101

Are there not dwellers in monasteries tempted, tormented, wrestling with phantoms created by their lust?

102

Sex is love only in a crude, groping, and primitive way. The experience it yields is but a faint distorted echo of love. The confusion of the original sound with its echo leads to delusion about both.

103

Sex wants to possess its beloved, even to enslave her. Love is willing to let her stay free. This is not an argument against marriage, for both sex and love can be found inside as well as outside marriage. It is an attempt to clear confusion and remove delusion.

104

To allow sex unlimited freedom is to destroy the possibility of higher attainment. There are physical, mental, and emotional disciplines to bring it under control. But to defeat it, the constant looking away, with joy, at the divine beauty, and frequent surrender to the divine stillness must complete them.

105

The love of the sexes will pose a hard problem for him. Along with physical regimes, he must find his solution by cold reasoning, austere disciplining, trained imagining, deep meditating, and devotional aspiring—a solution which must free him from the common state of either unsatisfied or over-satisfied desires. Only by probing to the very roots of this love and these desires, can he hope to bring them into accord with the philosophic ideal.

106

When the disciple has reached a certain stage, he will become clearly aware that the feeling of sexual lust, if it arises from time to time, is at times something out of his own past, not out of his present state, or an inheritance from parental tendencies impregnated in the body's nervous structure, or at other times something unconsciously transferred to him by another person. He will perceive vividly that what is happening is an *invasion* by an alien force—so alien that it will actually seem to be at some measurable distance from him, moving farther off as it weakens or coming closer as it strengthens. Therefore he will realize that the choice of accepting it as his own or rejecting it as not his own, is presented him. By refusing to identify himself with it, he quickly robs it of its power over him. The Buddha indeed gave an exercise to his disciples to defend themselves against such invasions by asking them to declare repeatedly, "This is not I. This is not mine."

107

The confusion between sexual pureness and sexual continence is widespread, fostered by the monastic traditions which interlace most religions. That we could be perfectly pure in mind without being perfectly chaste in body—that is, while yet remaining married—is not a conventional view.

108

The shame is not in sex but in abuse of it. Every man is loath to part with the sex relation and enter into the monastic state. Only sufficiently weighty counterbalancing forces will make him do so. We ought, therefore, to respect that state even if we feel no personal inclination to take the vow of chastity or see no theoretical necessity to do so.

109

In that moment of supreme sexual ecstasy, the most spiritually impoverished man gets a faded and fleeting glimpse of the love which inheres in the very nature of his higher Self. But whereas this glimpse merely torments him by its brevity and tantalizes him by its limited, faulty character, that higher impersonal love is eternal, unlimited, and supremely satisfying: it is indeed perfect love.

110

Since the first origin of the sexual instinct is ultimately traceable to the cosmic energy and since mystical joy immediately derives from contact with this energy, the conservation of one by the man who transmutes his passion, and the uprisal of the other, when he sends his forces in this direction, not only cancels all sense of loss but substitutes the divine for the animal. Both directions lead to ecstasy yet how rare and ethereal the one, how common and gross the other!

111

A truly philosophic attitude is neither ascetic nor hedonistic. It takes what is worthy from both—not by arithmetical computation to arrive at equal balance but by wise insight to arrive at harmonious living. It respects the creative vitality of man as something to be brought under control, and thereafter used conservatively or consciously sublimated. In this way the extreme points of view associated with fanaticism are rejected. The ridiculous results of such fanaticism can be heard in the nonsense talked equally by those who measure a man's spirituality by his monastic celibacy as well as by those who consider all celibacy unnecessary.

112

In our description of man it is not enough to mention his intellect and feelings, his intuition and will; we must not leave out his instincts and impulses. The sexual instinct, particularly, is of paramount importance.

113

The man who prefers the freedom but loneliness of celibacy to the companionship but chains of matrimony is entitled to do so.

114

The feminine component in the psyche is the passive, the inert, the element which yearns to be taken over and subjugated by another power. The male component is the active, the outgoing, that which aggressively drives out for release from its tensions.

115

He who can keep his chastity in thought and feeling not less than in conduct has reached a worthwhile achievement. He need not be ashamed of it nor hesitate to preserve it because of contrary counsel. It will do him no harm but can provide him with the power to sustain his highest endeavours. Not many can do this, it is true, and those whose physical continence is continually sapped by mental and emotional unchastity, might do better to follow Saint Paul's advice and marry rather than burn.

116

There is something terrifying in the mesmeric spell cast by sex, this vast universal power which lets the individual keep an illusion of personal initiative when all the time he is merely obeying its blind will.

117

If some cases of homosexuality come from the predominant carry-over of qualities brought from the opposite sex of the previous incarnation, others are an attempt by Nature at correcting the exaggerated development of those qualities, by birth in a body unable to express them properly.

118

The disillusionments about sex as it reveals the pain behind its pleasure, the ugliness behind its beauty, and the degradations behind its refinements mean nothing to the ordinary mind but must create a retreat from its urges in the superior mind.

119

All indulgence of the sexual instinct, beyond that needed for the deliberate procreation of wanted children, is really overindulgence. Every such expenditure of semen, which is the concentrated essence of physical life, is a wasting one.

120

A low-protein, raw food diet diminishes desires associated with the reproductive organ, but the result will last only as long as the diet lasts. A deliberate attempt to transmute these forces, made along mental, emotional, and spiritual directions, is also needed for more durable results.

121

The necessity of satisfying sexual lust—so prevalent in the ordinary man—disappears in the liberated person.

122

Lao Tzu said the man of Tao is free from the consciousness of sex.

123

If being and becoming, the world's inner reality and its outer appearance, are indeed one in the final ultimate view, then how can we cast out some functions of Nature as evil and yet retain others as good? Why should the passionless celibate be put on the highest grade of spirituality and the married man denied any entry if both are judged not by sexual activity or inactivity but by capacity to immolate the ego upon its funeral pyre?

124

If through the mystical Glimpse, God finds Himself temporarily in man's mind, through the creative act of love He finds Himself momentarily in man's body. Although this is but a poor echo of the other and higher discovery, muted and distorted and raucous by comparison, still it is in deepest meaning the union of self with Overself. In this lies its perpetual lure. But because it is a substitution, it is beset with miseries, frustrations, perils, and repulsions. And however often it is satisfied, neither the man nor the woman ever feels really fulfilled. This is because the inner need is ignored, the higher purpose not even thought of.

125

The five ascetic rules which Patanjali ordains for the yogi include, as their fourth item, *brahmacharya*. In India this term is usually taken to mean "abstinence from sexual intercourse; chastity," and is so translated into English. But the original esoteric and philosophic meaning is "restraint of the sexual forces." These two definitions are not identical.

126

Parenthood is not the only way for a man to express his creativeness. He may find other and useful channels for it. He may build a business or invent a machine, write a poem or help nature grow food or flowers.

127

If it is unwise for a young man who does not belong by nature to the strong-willed to embrace complete chastity, it is equally unwise for him, a quarter-century later, not to embrace it.

128

He who conserves his creative energy for the purpose of realizing his higher identity, will not at any time feel that he is suffering loss, privation, or torment. On the contrary, he will feel the gain of freedom, strength, and mastery.

129

The Sutra of the Forty-Two Sections (Chinese Mahayana):

Buddha said: "Of all longings and desires none is stronger than sex. Sex as a desire has no equal. Rely on the (universal) Oneness. No one is able to become a follower of the Way if he accepts dualism." The translator, "Chu Ch'an," comments: "The Buddhist argues that distinctions between this and that are really void and that fundamentally everything is one. Sex is an extreme example of the negation of this theory, since it depends entirely upon the attraction between opposites."

Buddha said: "To put a stop to these evil actions [unceasing indulgence of sexual passion] will not be so good as to put a stop to [the root] in your mind. If the mind desists, its followers will stop also."

130

His choice between celibacy and marriage must not only be circumstance-decided but, even more, intuitively guided. There are chaste persons who need to remain so. There are unchaste ones who need to become chaste. The sublimation of sex energy is the best ideal for both these classes. The first is set apart for this purpose by nature. The second must become strong enough to set themselves apart by deliberate decision. But the deep inner voice must be their counsel in this matter. For there are others who need the experience of married life, the subjection to its disciplines and temptations, the chance it offers to move away from egoism or to fall deeper into it.

131

The ascetic disciplines are often useful and necessary phases wherein to get rid of attachments to undesirable habits, remove impeding blockages, and get out of unhealthy conditions. But they are only phases of the quest, only means to an end. If they are overdone, or their place magnified and misunderstood, they create new blockages, attachments, and new cages from which the ascetic will later need to seek liberation. To condemn the human satisfactions, to reject pleasures, to brush aside the arts as irrelevant, is too sweeping, goes too far, and makes for unreasonableness.

132

If my earlier statements on sex seem to be contradicted in the later ones, the change must be admitted. For beginning as far back as *The Spiritual Crisis of Man*, I had stopped looking at the subject with the youthful rebellious eyes with which I had also looked at conventional society and religion. If Freud contributed to the earlier phase, it need not be thought that puritanism has done so to the later one.

133

The sex problem can only be settled by reference to the degree of evolution the individual has attained. To ask for complete celibacy from the beginner in the quest, however enthusiastic he may be, is to ask for confusion, unbalance, and possible disaster if he is still young and vigorous in body. It is better for him to pass through and outgrow what the ancient Hindus called "the householder stage" *before* he ventures into the saint's. Only the exceptional man can proceed direct to the higher stage and yet maintain his progress undisturbed.

134

It is unfortunate for such people—they are so numerous—but we are not here merely to be entertained, especially by sex; there are cosmic issues at play also.

135

A man may live celibately for years and be none the worse for it. Indeed he may be all the better. The effects will depend on his mental attitude, the kind of thoughts he has about it.

136

The body is not polluted by the presence of sexual organs as our ascetic friends seem to believe. Nature is wiser than they are. She knew what she was doing when she evolved them.

137

He need not make the reform in his habits of living until he is not only intellectually convinced of its need but also inwardly feels that the right time, the psychological moment, for it has arrived. In that way it will be unforced and natural, while its course and results will be lasting.

138

No woman can give man what she has not herself got. He can find perfect love only in the Overself which is above the fragmentariness of sex and completely whole in itself.

139

The Hindu religion put celibates on high-ranking pinnacles and admired those who practised asceticism. The Hebrew religion condemned celibacy and produced no ascetics. Yet both religions claimed divine inspiration.

140

The tantrik practice has been distorted in Northern India where, under the name of sahaja, a childless woman may approach a sadhu and request him to father her child. If he does so without seeking to experience pleasure, he is considered to be as moral and righteous and sinless as before!

141

The man who says, "I love you," too often means, "I want your body."

142

It is partly because women tend to be passive and receptive that they are more ready to believe in religion and more open to intuit mysticism than men are. But the price they often pay is to be less rational, less critical, more gullible. Hence they more easily become dupes of charlatanic or absurd cults.

143

Sex must be brought to heel, the illusions engendered by it must be exposed for what they really are. He will have to choose between abject unreflective surrender to a biological urge, grotesque over-evaluation of a glandular excitation on the one hand, and freedom, peace, and security on the other.

144

Trapped as they are in the limitations of this body, they seek compensation in freedom of the mind. But too many among the young have sought it wrongly—through the use of drugs, the abuse of alcohol, the forgetfulness in dissipated sex.

145

The romantic exchange of tender words between two young persons, whether still adolescent or a little older, with its stirring physical hormones and with or without gushing sentimentality, will be seen in a truer light after Nature has realized its purposes in them.

146

Some are called to chastity (which is a separate condition from celibacy). Others, uncertain, may try for it, and if unable to maintain it, acknowledge honourable defeat and are content with aspiration toward the lesser goals. Clearly a marriage for affinity and companionship, platonic, without physical love, is more difficult to realize but more suited to those who do not wish to forfeit the higher goals.

147

The pattern of succumbing to this overwhelming lust after a period of mounting tension and then feeling shame, regret, or revulsion, is a familiar one.

148

Whether freed from the demands of sex by the coming of old age or by the fulfilment of spiritual aspiration, he who enjoys this freedom can turn his mind more easily to the Peace within.

149

As regards sex, he should remember that if he is called by the Quest to give up everything for a time, or even for all time, it is only that he might receive something infinitely better in exchange. The Quest calls for renunciation of earthly desires, not to make him miserable, but to make him happy.

150

Outside of politics, on no subject about which it is possible to write is there likely to be so much criticism on the one side, and so much support on the other, as on the subject of sex. Sometimes a daring writer ventures to suggest that it is possible to advance by degrees in the inner life, and that it is not essential for the aspirants who are already married or for those who hope to get married eventually, to forswear the bliss and risk of wedded union. He is immediately corrected by rigidly chaste ladies and gentlemen in the West as well as not a few brown-robed monks in the East, who will sternly inform him that he has perverted the spiritual teaching and led these aspirants astray!

151

The Indian who remains a householder while following yoga, is expected to prepare himself before becoming a father, by four years of chastity.

152

The mere suppression of sex power does not lead to illumination but the redirection of it to a higher level may contribute, as one powerful factor, to such illumination.

153

All the forces of a man have to be mobilized in the search for higher consciousness. He cannot leave sex-force out, for example.

154

If they have a genuine vocation for the celibate life, they must honour it. But the young do not always know their own mind and sometimes this vocation is only an imaginary and false one. A temporary test will be helpful in finding out the truth of their fitness or unfitness for it.

155

There is but one end to such sensualism—unless it falls into still deeper self-deception—and that is disillusionment. The dancer Isadora Duncan's tragic cry before she died is instructive: "I have had as much as anyone of that sort of thing which men call love. Love?—rot! In the flesh there is no love."

156

Chastity will have been attained when he feels himself ready to take the sacred vow, not in response to some external bidding but rather to a strong internal one.

157

The end of these disciplines comes when both physical lust and emotional desire leave him completely. Their very root has then been destroyed. From that day he is useless to members of the opposite sex seeking either to make love or engender romance.

158

Whatever disciplined sex relation in marriage the Quester has allowed himself should itself be brought to an end when middle age is reached, for the practice of chastity is then as advisable both spiritually and physically as it is in youth. He needs to begin to untie himself from the worldly life and little by little withdraw into a more solitary, a more studious, a more abstemious and more meditative period.

159

The adolescent or the adult in whom this passion rises and seeks expression, will unavoidably be subject to mental conflict. It will not be ended without a struggle, often a protracted struggle which ceases only with the natural ebbing of energies that comes to the elderly or the sick. More rarely, it ceases when the man takes to the Quest and attains a far enough advancement on it. Some who pass through life without experiencing the struggle have either achieved the victory in earlier lives or have special physical causes to account for it. But where the struggle exists, one end result is to lead either to the enfeeblement or to growth of will.

160
The uprising of sexual desire is not due to sin but to Nature, which requires every being to balance the sex force. But where both the animal and the average man seek to do this through the body of a female, the illumined man is able to do it by sublimating the force inside himself.

161
Man attempts to complete himself in the momentary gratification of animal sex, or in the more lasting magnetic pairing of lifelong marriage.

162
Is chastity an indispensable condition for the quester? Celibacy, a virtue to Catholic priesthood, a vice to Muhammedan doctors of religious law, is neither to the Quest.

163
A Chinese gentleman who belonged to a high official's family in the pre-Communist regime and who went to Tibet in search of wisdom and a master, spent eight years in a famous monastery in the latter country. He lived as a monk, studied and meditated under the advanced teachers, and was honoured with a title for his excellence in Buddhist learning. But in the end he left Tibet, got married, and had children. He told me that he felt there were weaknesses in his character which had to be worked out in a householder's life. He was honest and truthful. But how many monks did he leave behind in the monastery who had taken the vows, as he did, in their twenties and were now struggling with their sexual thoughts in secret?

164
Emmett Fox, who wrote some widely circulated little books on positive thinking, was able to fill Carnegie Hall, New York, to capacity whenever he lectured there. He was a tall good-looking man and attracted the admiration of women, but he kept himself aloof and reserved from them. One of his followers, an unmarried lady in her late thirties, became infatuated with him to the point of complete helplessness. Finally she had to confess her love to him. He stood up behind her, placed one hand on her hand and the other on the back of her neck. She felt kundalini force being drawn up the spine to her head. Thereafter she was free of this sexual obsession.

165
The biological attraction of the sexes normally has its zenith and its nadir. This statement is true despite that it seems belied by today's facts. For the exceptions arise either from artificial stimulation and deliberate suggestion through modern arts or through the perversion of Nature— including its surgical perversion—or possession of the body by disincarnate spirits or the use of practices which are little known and perilous.

166
Washing the organs concerned with cold water once or twice a day helps to get free from the congestion of blood in the vessels there.

167
The titillation of a gland joined to the stimulation of a number of nerves is pleasurable and tempts men to repeat the experience. If this repetition is pushed to excess, they become stupefied and fall into a pit dug by their own hands.

168
It is not all sects of tantra which seek either to delay the act of ejaculation or to prevent it altogether, but it is certainly the higher ones. There are others who have brought all tantrism into disrepute because of their debased practices.

169
The act of union is not in itself a polluting one, for it is part of Nature's process. But pollution sets in when the act is abused, misused, degraded, or perverted. Where pollution does not exist, discipline or rejection of the act is enjoined because of the tremendous immersion in, and concentration upon, the physical body, which it causes.

170
The snake crawling on its belly is as close to the earth as any animal could get. As a symbol this creature stands in ancient scriptures for earthly pleasure. And since there is no pleasure so intense as the sexual one, it has come to stand for that particularly. The snake rearing its head and holding itself upright stands for the overcoming of sexual passion. It is not only a symbol of such mastery but particularly of the power arising from its being diverted toward spiritual knowledge and aspiration.

171
Explain the original single-sexed nature of the human being, what the division into two sexes entails, why the problems of sex become more complicated with the evolution of the human being, and the impossibility of giving a satisfactory rule for sexual behaviour to all seekers and why it must be adjusted to the varying stages and circumstances of individual seekers. State the ultimate goal which all have to attain eventually. Point out (a) the dangers of premature monastic celibacy so far as it affects the

next incarnation, and (b) the dangers of overstimulation of sex in modern civilization. Explain how those who seek to curb or control sex desire may get help from the physical disciplines. Breeding children is a duty which cannot be prescribed for all but depends upon individual circumstances, natural inclination, and evolutionary stage.

172

The seeking of pleasure through sex necessarily brings him close to the edge of an enfeebled will, a sinking in physical being, and an entanglement in mere animality. More than this, the energies thus spent or lost are the concentrated essence of his human being—bodily, emotional, and mental. If these energies are controlled, directed, and uplifted to a higher plane altogether, they become the source, no longer of spiritual degradation, but of spiritual development.

173

Can men and women love each other only pornographically? Can their two egos find no better point of contact than the one which makes them no better than apes?

174

The lustful libertine, whose prayer is, "Give us this day our daily bed," will shrink with horror from any such discipline.

175

In this mutual surrender and ecstatic merger of one individual to another that is sexual love, we may see both a reflection and a symbol of the higher union of the ego with the Overself.

176

The desperation with which they fight this inescapable part of their nature in the struggle for a pseudo-virtue, the enormous physiological and spiritual ignorance in which such fighting is usually involved, leads to a lot of needless suffering.

177

The monkish outlook which deprecates the life of a householder and exaggerates the necessity of strict celibacy, is expressed in a large part of mystical literature. But this is only because the authors were monks and nuns themselves, or lay persons trained by monks and nuns, or old men and women who had little sympathy with the feelings and needs of younger ones. Such antagonism towards sex is all the more confusing since it is as much justified by some of the facts as it is refuted by others.

178

The Buddha pointed out that giving reality to an illusion so powerful as the sexual force makes men see as attractive what, to reason, is repulsive. It is a magical force.

179

That aspirant has attained purity who no longer desires any human being but only pure Being itself. Thus he passes from the personal to the impersonal, from passion through penitence and self-discipline to utter tranquillity.

180

The minority which is able and willing to practise complete chastity and finds its way into convents and monasteries shows by its smallness how hard and how unattractive that virtue is.

181

It is not necessary to limit sex-transmuting only to kundalini-raising exercise. The mind can be directed toward affirmations of sex control when doing most of the stretching and bending exercises.

182

Flirt before forty, if you must, and philosophize after it, would seem to be a rule followed by too many modern people. Fortunately, some will find better things to do in a better age than to spend their swift-passing years in seeking to attract amatory attentions. They may then be able to pause and think for a while as to why they incarnated. Flippant flirtation is certainly a pleasant mode of passing time, but it is not an activity that can be continued into the sixties and seventies of one's life. And those who become aware of this certainty in advance will not find life becoming an unutterable and unbearable bore as they become older, as do the others.

183

Sex is like a double-edged sword. On the one hand it may bring the keenest enjoyment, but on the other the keenest pain. Therefore, it is to be wielded prudently, carefully, sanely, and with understanding.

184

There are periods in an aspirant's life when he is called to the discipline of utter chastity—and such a period may last for years or a lifetime, depending on each individual's particular circumstance. But until the call comes, preceding periods need not be so tightly disciplined. In short, his life will follow a rhythm of cycles. There are some who are called by their nature to an entire lifetime of utter chastity. It is easy and natural and right for them to be monks. But they are few. The others will do better to enter the marriage relation and are so formed by nature to need it. Both groups should avoid the fanaticism which wrongly insists on demanding that all others conform to their particular type. But this said, the ultimate ideal must still be left in view. It is always advisable in this Quest to discipline sex passions so as to become eventually independent of them. At a certain stage, complete chastity has to be observed and firmly established. Until then, anything he can do to make his emotional nature as pure as his strength will allow helps in every way. He should let all his longing and desires gradually converge on this single longing and desire for union with the Overself. He can utilize odd moments for kindling and rekindling this one yearning. The stronger it becomes, the greater will be the descent of Grace at the initiation periods.

8

KUNDALINI

At opposing ends of the spine, the human and the animal oppose each other.(P)

2

Why did so many primeval cultures in Asia, Africa, and America worship the serpent? A full answer would contain some of the most important principles of metaphysics and one of the least known practices of mysticism—raising the force symbolized under the name of the "serpent fire." The advanced occultists of Tibet compare the aspirant making this attempt to a snake which is made to go up a hollow bamboo. Once aroused, it must either ascend and reach liberty at the top or it must fall straight down to the bottom. So he who seeks to play with this fiery but dangerous power will either reach Nirvana or lose himself in the dark depths of hell. If a man seeks to arouse kundalini before he has rid himself of hate, he will only become the victim of his own hatreds when he does raise it from its sleeping state. He would do better to begin by self-purification in every way if he is to end in safety and with success. The uprising of the penis closely resembles the uprearing of the cobra. Both become erect and stiff by their own innate force. When the serpent fire passes from the root of the penis up the spinal cord, the latter also becomes upright and stiff. Yet sex is not the serpent power but the chief one of its several expressions. The advanced yogis of India symbolize by the pent-up hissing of the serpent the aggressive energy of this sex power. They picture the threefold character of the process in their texts as a triangle with a serpent coiled up inside it. The intense fire of love for the higher self must be kindled in the "mystic" heart, kindled until it also shows a physical parallel in the body, until the latter's temperature rises markedly and the skin perspires profusely. Deep breathing is an important element in this exercise. It provides in part the dynamism to make its dominating ideas effective. The other part is provided by a deliberate sublimation of sex energy, through its imaginative raising from the organs in the lower part of the body to a purified state in the head.

The strange phenomena of a mysterious agitation in the heart and an internal trembling in the solar plexus, of sex force raised through the spine to the head in intense aspiration toward the higher self accompanied by deep breathing, of a temporary consciousness of liberation from the lower nature, are usually the forerunners of a very important step forward in the disciple's inner life. A twofold trembling may seize him. Physically, his diaphragm may throb violently, the movement spreading like a ripple upward to the throat. Emotionally, his whole being may be convulsed with intense sobbing. It is this same bodily agitation, this nervous repercussion of a higher emotional upheaval, which developed in the meetings of the early members of the Society of Friends and got them the name of Quakers. The agitation of his feeling will come to an end with the calm perception of his Soul. The kundalini's activity being primarily mental and emotional, the diaphragmatic tremors and quivers are merely its physical reactions. The necessity for keeping the back erect exists only in this exercise, not in the devotional or intellectual yogas, for such a straight posture permits the spinal column to remain free for the upward passage of the "serpent fire." The latter moves in spiral fashion, just like the swaying of a cobra, generating heat in the body at the same time. If the trembling continues long enough and violently enough, a sensation of heat is engendered throughout the body and this in turn engenders profuse perspiration. But all these symptoms are preliminary and the real mystical phenomena involving withdrawal from the body-thought begin only when they have subsided. This exercise first isolates the force residing in breath and sex, then sublimates and reorients it. The results, after the initial excitement has subsided, are (a) a liberating change in his consciousness of the body, (b) a strengthening development of the higher will's control over the animal appetites, and (c) a concentration of attention and feeling as perfect as a snake's concentration on its prey. It is a threefold process yielding a threefold result. In those moments when the force is brought into the head, he feels himself to be liberated from the rule of animality; then he is at the topmost peak of the higher will. Power and joy envelop him. The attainment of this state of deep contemplation and its establishment by unremitting daily repetition bring him finally to an exalted satisfied sense of being full and complete and therefore passion-free and peace-rooted.(P)

3

The attempt to gain all or nothing and to gain it at once might succeed on the stock exchange but is hardly likely to succeed here. He cannot leap abruptly to this great height across the intervening stages but must travel laboriously step by step upwards to it. Nevertheless there exists a way of taking the kingdom by violence, a way which can be finished in six months. It is the arousal of the serpent fire. But unless the nature has been well purified, it may prove a highly dangerous way. Few are yet ready for it, and no teacher dare incur the responsibility of plunging into such a risky gamble with his pupil's health, sanity, morality, and spiritual future unless there is sufficient sexual stability and hardness of will in him. There is a slower way, the yoga of self-identification with the Guru. Practised once or twice daily, and combined with Mantramjapa practised continuously, it leads to the same goal in a period twelve times as long and is perfectly safe. He should understand that the goal both ways lead to is not the philosophic one. Yet to attain the latter it is indispensable to pass through the mystic's goal. From all this we may gather not only how long is the road, but also how grand is the achievement with which philosophy is concerned.(P)

4

Time, space, and sex, which limit and make him captive, can also be used to serve and set him free. The mind can take time and slow it down by slowing down the procession of thoughts (yoga) and take space by holding the body immobile during the same work, so that both phases assist toward the success of the yoga. It can take sex and drive the inherent force of it, helped by breath and concentration, up the spinal column to the heart and brain, transmuting it by eliminating its cry of loneliness.

5

What the Hindus call *kundalini*, meaning the "coiled force," is really a manifestation of this power of the Overself. It does not necessarily have to appear in the case of every progressing disciple; but where it does, it is as if an uncoiled force moves rapidly up the spine and passes out through the head, whereupon the meditator involuntarily enters the deep trance condition for a while.

6

It is much easier to awaken spirit-energy than to deliberately divert it by drawing it up to the head as transformed spiritual power. It is a necessary precondition for this awakening that the body be purified and no less so the character.

7

The awakening of serpent fire gives a tremendous stimulation to the nervous system. There may be difficulty in sleeping as a result.

8

Not all yogas make so much of the quality of peace as an object to be secured by their means: there is one which makes even more of power. It frankly seeks enhancement of the spiritual and psychical *energies*, as well as the acquisition of new ones. Their exploitation leads to the diverse powers and "gifts of the Spirit."

9

The power which is felt is what the Hindus call *kundalini*, and it is gradually generated over the many years through which he practised meditation and sublimated sex. Usually when allowed to pass out of the head it leads to a spiritual experience of ecstatic illumination, but of course that can be done only when it is accepted without fear and in full faith. Its activity sometimes interferes with sleep for several months, but not usually longer.

10

After the Spirit-Energy awakes and begins to mount up the trunk, a double sensation is felt. From the meditator's own breathing, thinking, and willing activities, he himself seems to be pushing the force upwards. But from what he also experiences psychically and intuitively, something overhead seems to be magnetically pulling his head up and elongating his body and drawing the Spirit-Energy up to itself. The two influences do not counterbalance each other but prevail alternatively by turns.

11

In the Hindu *chakra* system (of which you can see gaudy coloured lithographs in the yogic circles of India) the lowest and first centre deals with survival, the second with sex, the third with power. Thus the first three are animalistic, egoistic, and materialistic; but when we come to the fourth there is a crossing over, for this has to do with spiritualization. The fifth is connected with surrender of the ego, and the sixth with the discrimination between truth and falsity, between reality and appearance. The seventh is the last and highest and is linked with enlightenment, liberation, realization—call it what you will. But all this applies to the particular yoga called *kundalini* yoga. Philosophy is not concerned with it, because it is not *directly* concerned with the awakening of *kundalini*.

12

The Spirit-Energy: What are the lines of connection between the Over-self and the body?

The first can be traced to thoughts. These express themselves through, and are in turn conditioned by, the physical brain and the spinal nerve system.

The second can be traced to emotions. These express themselves through, and are also conditioned by, the solar plexus and the sympathetic nerve system.

The third line can be traced to the vital forces. Although these permeate every organ of the body, and express themselves through every cell of it, they are specially centered in the heart, lungs, and genitals.

These three connections can plainly be seen. But they are not the whole. There is still a fourth line, although it cannot be traced in a manner acceptable to the sciences of anatomy and physiology, and very little is known about it anyway. The Indian yogis have named it variously: the Serpent Power, the Snake Force, World Energy. The Christian mystics have named it the Holy Ghost and the Pentecostal Power. To the monks of famed Mount Athos it is "the Athos Light"; to Saint John it was "the light of men;" and to Saint Luke, "the light of the body." The Chinese mystics have named it the Circulating Light.

It is really nothing other than the soul's Energy, the dynamic aspect of the still centre hidden deep in man. Its first activity is traceable in psychical and intuitive experiences outside the normal range as well as in abnormal physical phenomena; its final one is the supreme mystical experience which throws out awareness of the body altogether.

Thus through thought and feeling, physical vitality and spiritual vitality, there occurs a mutual interaction between the soul and flesh. Each affects the other. Each can, in abnormal conditions, affect the other even so dramatically as to appear miraculous in its power over the other.

The seven chief endocrine glands of the human body are associated with psychic centres in or near the spinal structure not visible to the physical eye. When the "Spirit-Force" is brought by the power of aspiration into the first centre, which is associated with the sacral gland, the body's vitality is markedly increased and its resistance to disease correspondingly increased too. The Hindu's texts picture it under the symbol of a lotus flower with four luminous petals.

With the entry of this energy into the second centre, associated with the prostate gland in men and the ovarian gland in women, the nervous system is strengthened, resistance to nervous disorders correspondingly increased, ability to concentrate mentally enhanced, and a resolute determination to rise up and succeed in some chosen endeavour manifested. In the third centre, associated with the adrenal gland, the power to influence other people's minds and even, to some extent, to heal them of sickness is developed. Along with this, the quality of fearlessness shows itself to an extraordinary degree. In the fourth centre, associated with the thymus gland, the "Spirit-Energy" ascends to the region of the heart and with that consciousness touches a higher plane of being. There is a progressive thinning down of egoism. With the fifth centre, associated with the thyroid gland, the emotions are at last balanced by, and poised in, the intuition. Along with this development, the illusion of time is banished. This gives a feeling of agelessness. Physically it bestows an improved power of speech in the sense that it becomes creative, forceful, and illuminating to its hearers. With the sixth centre, associated with the pituitary gland in the frontal region of the head, creative power is bestowed upon the concentrated Will and the spoken or written Word. With the seventh centre, associated with the pineal gland at the base of the brain, the illusion of the ego's reality is shattered, and the true self, or soul, is discovered. The ancient Indian books symbolize it in the form of a lotus with one thousand petals. The immense contrast of this with the small number of four of the first centre is intended to show that here at last is full and final illumination.

13

He must redirect the generative power, raising it upward mentally and willing its transmutation intensely. This is the moment to express command over the lower nature and to exert obedience from the lesser faculties.

14

This Spirit-fire is to be brought from the perineum along the spinal column to the topmost point in the head. Such a passage is not accomplished all at once, but only by stages—seven in all. At the entry into each stage there is a tremendous agitation of feeling and thought and a vibrant ecstasy of dominating power.

15

The Sacral Plexus, at the spine's base and in the pelvic region, stores procreative power. If this power is stored for a sufficient length of time, and if it is undisturbed by sexual passions and kindred emotions during that time, and if there is a deliberate redirection in higher channels, whether they be the strengthening of the body and development of its muscles, or whether they be the achievement of professional ambitions or the unfoldment of spiritual qualities, transmutation will take place.

16

This explains why the old Sanskrit texts say the Spirit-Energy brings the yogi to his freedom but puts the universe into bondage. What other bondage could be meant than sexual slavery?

17

He who brings to the attempt a sufficient degree of informed spiritual development and mental-emotional self-control need have no fear. But he who does not—and such a type is in the majority—may find the solar plexus pouring the force unrestrainedly through his nervous system, inducing permanent insomnia by reason of its pressure upon his brain, until his mind becomes unhinged.

18

Those who awaken this Energy before they are in a position adequately to control it, put themselves in peril. For should they yield to temptation and misuse it to serve their lower nature or to harm other persons, it will return like an Australian boomerang to punish them.

19

Since sex is so near to the earlier manifestation of Spirit-Energy, it must be controlled and sublimated *before* that Energy is deliberately aroused, as the danger of becoming obsessed by sex is a serious one.

20

A current of electricity charging powerfully through the body is the nearest experience to it.

21

When the Spirit-Energy enables him to help others, he may see them surrounded by phosphorescent greyish-blue light.

22

They are really brain centres, although of a minor character compared with the great brain in the head. They are situated both in the cerebro-spinal nerve system and in the sympathetic one. The entry of Spirit-Energy into them energizes them and activates their psycho-spiritual functions.

23

This force lies within him, latent and unused, until he turns to the exercises and disciplines of the Quest.

24

The introduction of nicotine in appreciable quantities by smoking bars the way to the Spirit-Energy's movement and clogs the centres it would ordinarily open. The introduction of alcohol in similar quantities by drinking gives a wrong direction to the Energy so that its benefits are lost. From this we see how important for other than all the usual and well-known reasons is the ascetic self-discipline which limits or denies the use of these two poisons.

25

The creative force is to be drawn up by will and mind and breath from the sexual organ to the heart and to the brain alternately. These three mediums are to be united in the single endeavour.

26

The region of the solar plexus is a sensitive receiving set into which the emotional forces of the lower nature can, by concentrating with the mind, be drawn. Here they are purified and driven upwards by a determined will and a deepened breath to the region of the heart. If this is successfully done, the "Spirit-Energy" may be aroused, with momentous consequences. A sense of well-being will be diffused through the trunk of the body and a feeling of happiness will arise in the emotions themselves.

27

In some of its aroused phases the Spirit-Energy is quite resistless; therefore a purified and disciplined life is essential before releasing it.

28

Oriental traditions speak of certain psychonervous centres situated near the plexuses of the physical body which are not physical themselves and hence are part of an invisible body or aura emanating from the physical one.

29

The defect of arousing the Energy by breathing exercises is that the effects finally wear off and leave the man without his powers. A permanent result cannot be obtained by this method. That is why hatha yogis are warned not to wait too long before taking the next step higher.

30

The Egyptians signified the Spirit-Energy by a winged snake, and the Nepalese by a trumpeting elephant in a triangle.

31

When the upward flow of the force brings it to the pineal gland, which is located in the sympathetic nervous system and inside the brain, and when other requirements are complied with, the gland is energized and activated and gives man spiritual vision.

32

There is a stage in the disease of "progressive" syphilis (which is much harder to cure than ordinary syphilis) where the sufferer may have illusions of personal grandeur and be swept off his feet by egocentric ideas arising from his mental deterioration and unbalance. Hitler was one such sufferer. There is another curious fact about syphilis, and that is the course followed by the disease in the body itself. This course is identical with the path followed by the Serpent-Power (*kundalini*) as it moves upward from the sex centre to the brain centre, where it gives the true enlightenment. The imaginary enlightenment of a syphilitic dictator is thus its counterfeit satanic copy.

33

Such is the power of this Spirit-Energy that in the case of Padre Pio, the stigmatist, his bodily temperature in earlier years would rise on certain special occasions to such a high temperature that the thermometer could not measure it and would break!

34

The vagus nerve is part of the central nervous system and extends from the brain all the way down to the solar plexus. It actually traces the path of the kundalini moving on its return course.

35

Once this dormant energy is aroused, a man's whole nature begins to change. He begins to reform habits, engage in more regular and deeper meditations, move forward by determined efforts toward the mastery of his whole being.

36

Patanjali says, "This light shines from within only when all the impurities of the heart have been removed by practice of Yoga."

37

The Spirit-Energy is a fiery power. The yogis say it *burns* its way as it spirals through the body.

38

These exercises bring about a better flow of the body's vital force. When this force is blocked or impeded at any point, trouble appears there. The exercises open the blockages.

39

When the Spirit-Energy touches the heart, an exhilarating and ecstatic freedom is felt, a deep and boundless delight.

40

Ordinarily, it comes to birth very, very slowly, as the exercises are practised and the purifications are undergone; but, in quite a number of cases, it comes up with a sudden rush.

41

Kundalini is the driving force of sex. It is the original life-force *behind* all human activity—mental and physical, spiritual as well as sexual—because it was behind the very birth of the human entity itself.

42

The force is constructively raised from the genital organs by progressive stages upward to the pineal gland in the brain and then to the pituitary gland in the forehead.

43

The serpent fire starts at the sex organs, proceeds to the solar plexus as the most important ganglion of the sympathetic nerve system, continues up the spine and ends in the frontal brain. These are the progressive stations of its passage when governed by will and directed by aspiration. The first sign is an increase of the heat of the body, sometimes resulting in perspiration. The second sign of its movement is a trembling or agitation in the navel region of the abdomen as the solar plexus is entered and the magnetic centre within it begins to open. The third sign is an unconscious drawing of deeper breaths. The last sign is a sensation of added force on all levels—physical, emotional, mental, and mystical.

44

The creative energy is one and the same no matter how high or how low may be the level upon which it manifests and how refined or how gross the form through which it expresses itself.

45

This force is originally derived from the sun. It is universal, living, conscious, and like electricity in its dynamic potency. Its appearance in the sex energy is but one, and that the very lowest, of its appearances. Just as each member of the sound, light, heat, electricity and magnetism group is either convertible into one of the others or able to bring it into existence, so this solar force is convertible from sex, when governed, to higher and still higher forms.

9

POSTURES FOR PRAYER

The body can make its contributions, too, in this work of a spiritual aspirant following the religious path—the path of devotion and worship and prayer—rather than the yogic path of mental control and mental silence. I have devised a series of physical attitudes to be used in what I have called Philosophical Prayer, so that each different kind of prayer has its corresponding position of the body. For such a person the attitudes assumed physically in prayer are important because they help the work of inducing the feelings and thoughts appropriate to each kind. For others, who wish to follow the yogic path, there is, of course, the way of hatha yoga as a means of bringing the body into obedience to the will and aspiration while seeking to bring the thoughts into concentration and under control. This, too, this hatha yoga, has its own physical postures and breath rhythms, its way of sitting or squatting, its tensions and relaxations.

2

The Seven Sacred Physical Postures and Mental Attitudes of Philosophic Worship (Essay)

The function of these postures is suggestive and helpful. They are symbolic of seven emotional attitudes. Each physical posture is to some extent an index to the feelings which actuate it. Because man dwells in a body of flesh, his bodily posture is as significant during prayer and worship as during any other activity: it becomes a sacred gesticulation.

Some mystically minded people, either because they reject all ceremonial observance or because they can see no utility in them whatever, object to using these postures. On the first ground, we answer that in philosophy such practices are not hollow rites, but valuable techniques, if performed with consciousness and with intelligent understanding. On the second ground, we answer that the exercises depolarize the physical body's earthward gravitation and render it more amenable to the entrance of spiritual currents. They clear the aura of undesirable magnetism. If anyone feels that he has no need of them, he may dispense with them.

Three remarks by Avicenna serve as an excellent introduction to use of these postures.

"The act of prayer should further be accompanied by those attitudes and rules of conduct usually observed in the presence of kings: humility, quietness, lowering the eyes, keeping the hands and feet withdrawn, not turning about and fidgeting."

"These postures of prayer, composed of recitation, genuflection, and prostration and occurring in regular and definite numbers, are visible evidence of that real prayer which is connected with, and adherent to, the rational soul. In this manner the body is made to imitate that attitude, proper to the soul, of submission to the Higher Self, so that through this act man may be distinguished from the beasts."

"And now we would observe that the outward, disciplinary part of prayer, which is connected with personal motions according to certain numbered postures and confined elements, is an act of abasement, and of passionate yearning on the part of this lower, partial, compound, and limited body towards the lunary sphere."

—from *Avicenna on Theology*,
by A.J. Arberry

1. *Standing and remembrance.*

(a) Stand comfortably, facing towards the east or the sun. (b) Plant the feet ten inches apart, raise arms forward and upward until they are about halfway between vertical and horizontal levels, at forty-five degrees above the horizontal, and fully extended. (c) The palms of both hands should be turned away and upward. (d) The head is slightly raised and the eyes are uplifted.

Bring the mind's attention abruptly away from all other activities and concentrate only on the Higher Power, whether as God, the Overself, or the Master. The act of uplifting the arms should synchronize with decisively uplifting the thoughts. The mere fact of abruptly abandoning all activities and of practising the lifting of hands for a certain time will help to bring about the uplift of the mind.

2. *Stretching and worship.*

(a) Assume the same position of feet and arms as in the previous posture. (b) Bend in lower part of arms at elbows and bring palms of both hands flatly together, at the same time inhaling deeply. Hold the breath a few seconds. Exhale while letting arms fall.

The attitude should be one of loving, reverential, adoring worship of the Overself.

3. *Bowing and aspiration.*

(a) With feet still apart, place both hands lightly on front of the thighs. (b) Bend the trunk forward at the waistline until it is nearing a horizontal level. Take care to keep both knees rigidly straight and unbent. (c) Let the palms slide downward until they touch the knees. Relax the fingers. (d) The head should be in line with the backbone, with the eyes looking down to the floor.

By pouring the devotion and love towards the Higher Power, the feeling of a personal relation to It should be nurtured.

4. *Kneeling and confessions.*

(a) Drop down to the floor and rest the knees upon it. (b) Lift the trunk away from the heels, keeping it in a straight erect line with the thighs. (c) Flatten the palms of both hands together and bring them in front of, as well as close to, the breast. (d) Close the eyes. This, of course, is the traditional Christian prayer posture.

Remorsefully acknowledge weaknesses in character and confess sins in conduct in a repentant, self-humbling attitude. Be quite specific in naming them. Also confess the limitations, deficiencies, and imperfections one is aware of. Second, ask for strength from the Higher Power to overcome those weaknesses, for light to find Truth, and for Grace. The qualities needed to counteract them should be formulated in definite terms. This confession is an indispensable part of the philosophic devotions. When it is sincere and spontaneous, it makes a proud man humble and thus opens the first gate in the wall of Grace. It compels him to become acutely conscious of his ignorance and ashamedly aware of his weakness. The praying person humbles the ego and breaks up his vanity; therefore he must not hide his mistakes or look for excuses. Only through such frankness can the time come when he will get the strength to overcome that mistake. This confession forces the praying person down to the ground and his self-respect with him, like a humiliated beggar. In his anguish, he constantly rediscovers his insufficiency and need of help from God or God's man.

5. *Squatting and submission.*

(a) Remaining on the knees, sink down until both heels support the trunk's weight, spine and head erect, hands on thighs. (b) Lower the chin until it touches the chest. (c) The eyes should be kept half-closed.

This posture is to be done with the mind and heart together completely emptied and surrendered to the Higher Power in utter resignation of the self-will. Humbly surrender the ego and discard its pride. Pray for Grace and ask to be taken up into the Overself completely. It is a sound instinct which causes a man to bend his head when the feeling of reverence becomes strong within him.

6. *Prostrating and union.*

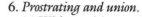

(a) Without rising, and keeping legs folded at the knees, bend the torso forward and incline the face as low as possible. (b) Bring the hands to rest upon the floor-rug, with palms outstretched, taut, and touching. (c) Place the forehead upon the hands. The knees should then be crouched up toward the chest. All ten toes must touch the floor. (d) Shut the eyes. The ancient Egyptian religion made "hetbu" or "bowing to the ground" an important part of its worship. The Muhammedans make bowings of the body during prayer equally important. This posture is practised widely in the Orient, but it is inconvenient to most Western people and is therefore usually withdrawn from them. If anyone, however, is much attracted to it, he may practise it.

During this posture, one should empty the mind of all thoughts and still 'it. Relax the emotions, open the heart, and be completely passive, trying to feel the inflow of heavenly love, peace, and blessing.

7. *Gesturing* (with thoughts concentrated on service and self-improvement).

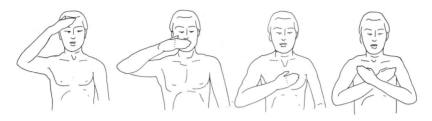

(a) So as not to lose this high mood, rise from the floor slowly and smoothly to resume ordinary activities in the world. At the same time, turn attention away from self towards others, if inclined. Intercede for them, draw blessings down upon them, and hold them up to the divine light, power, and peace. (b) Press the right hand to brow, mouth, and heart by turns, pausing at each gesture. Resolve to follow firmly the ideal qualities mentioned during the confession of posture 4. When touching the brow, resolve to do so in thoughts; when touching the mouth, resolve to do so in speech; and when touching the heart, resolve to do so in feelings.

Epilogue.

Cross and fold the arms diagonally while standing. The hands will then rest upon the chest, the fingers will point upwards toward the shoulders. In this last stage, you are to be sincerely thankful, joyously grateful, and constantly recognizant for the fact that God *is*, for your own point of contact with God, and for the good—spiritual and material—that has come your way.

Index for Part 2

Entries are listed by chapter number followed by "para" number. For example, 7.70 means chapter 7, para 70, and 3.47, 49, 115, etc., means chapter 3, paras 47, 49, 115, etc. Chapter listings are separated by a semicolon. Please note also that, for the reader's convenience, the first number in the right-hand running heads throughout the text indicates chapter number.

A

abstinence 7.70, 86; *see also* celibacy; chastity
adrenal gland 8.12
Albigenses 3.3
alcohol 2.56; 3.47, 49, 115, 120; 4.20; 7.114
  and breath exercises 6.37
  intolerance towards 3.43; 7.70
  as medicine 3.49
  and meditation 1.1 (p. 4); 3.80
  as obstacle to kundalini 8.24
  overcoming desire for 3.26, 56, 137, 143; 7.70
  and spiritual progress 3.56, 114
Alexander, F. Messias 2.66
allergies 3.133
animals
  evolution of 3.58
  hunting of 3.51, 90, 108, 144
  included in World-Idea 3.101
  kindness to 3.58
Anthony, Saint 3.162
Arab mystics, and fasting 4.43
Arberry, A.J. 9.2
arthritis, treatment for 4.59
asceticism 7.6, 131
  vs. discipline 3.137
  fanatical 2.21, 80, 84
  as necessary purification 4.23
  philosophic 2.34
Aschner, Dr. 4.59

B

Atlantis 3.101
  system of physical exercise 5.72
aura 8.28
  and posture 9.2
Aurobindo, Sri 2.85–86
Avicenna 9.2
avocado 3.140

back problems 5.45; *see also* spine
Backster, Cleve 3.63
balance, in diet 3.126, 129, 161
baths 4.49, 51–52
beans 3.139, 168
Beethoven, Ludwig van 2.7
Bey, Tahra 1.1 (p. 7)
Bey, Hamid 1.1 (p. 7)
Bhagavad Gita, on diet 3.82, 93, 168
Bible 6.40
  and vegetarianism 3.123, 134
bicycle rides 7.61
birth, second, outer physical results 2.99
Blavatsky, Madame Helena, and cigarettes 3.183
Bodhidharma 3.52
Bose, Sir J. 3.63
bowing, and aspiration 9.2
brahmacharya 7.125
Brahmananda, Swami 3.183
bread 2.13; 3.52, 163
breakfast 4.59

The 28 Categories from the Notebooks

This outline of categories in *The Notebooks* is the most recent one Paul Brunton developed for sorting, ordering, and filing his written work. The listings he put after each title were not meant to be all-inclusive. They merely suggest something of the range of topics included in each category.

1 THE QUEST

   Its choice —Independent path —Organized groups —
   Self-development —Student/teacher

2 PRACTICES FOR THE QUEST

   Ant's long path —Work on oneself

3 RELAX AND RETREAT

   Intermittent pauses —Tension and pressures —Relax body,
   breath, and mind —Retreat centres —Solitude —
   Nature appreciation —Sunset contemplation

4 ELEMENTARY MEDITATION

   Place and conditions —Wandering thoughts —Practise
   concentrated attention —Meditative thinking —
   Visualized images —Mantrams —Symbols
   —Affirmations and suggestions

5 THE BODY

   Hygiene and cleansings —Food —Exercises and postures
   —Breathings —Sex: importance, influence, effects

6 EMOTIONS AND ETHICS

   Uplift character —Re-educate feelings —Discipline emotions —
   Purify passions —Refinement and courtesy —Avoid fanaticism

7 THE INTELLECT

   Nature —Services —Development —Semantic training —
   Science —Metaphysics —Abstract thinking

8 THE EGO

   What am I? —The I-thought —The psyche